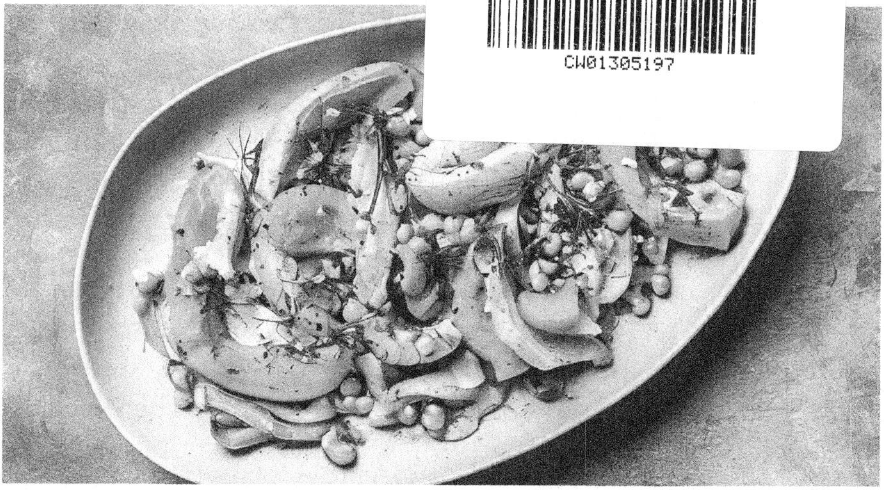

Thanks for Picking up this Book

Hi and welcome to a new way of cooking to reduce your UPF consumption. If you're reading this you've probably started your journey towards reducing your intake of Ultra-Processed Food (UPF) but for those of you to whom this is new, here's some info on what Ultra-Processed Foods are and why many of us are choosing to reduce our intake of them or cut them out completely. Before we delve deeper, I'd like to take a short moment to acknowledge that each of us has a hierarchy of food needs.

A great illustration of this can be found by looking up the work of Ellyn Satter. This pyramid of food needs begins with attaining "enough food" before moving on to "good tasting food" and eventually to "instrumental food" where not only is the quantity, quality and variety of food considered but also whether the food is "good for you". It's important to remember that everyone lives in a different food environment and is subject to different levels of pressure and stress related to nourishing themselves. If you are feeling anxious about the food you eat or what you feed others then first please give yourself some space to understand this. Remember that even a small step in the right direction is a positive action. You may not be able to change everything overnight, such is the food landscape in which we find ourselves, but each small change can help you move towards your goal - whatever that may be.

Now, what is UPF? UPF or Ultra-Processed Food, refers to food products that have undergone extensive processing, often involving industrial techniques and the addition of various additives and food processing aids. These foods typically contain a myriad of artificial flavours, colours, preservatives, and other additives to enhance taste, texture, and shelf life. Common ingredients in UPF include refined sugars, hydrogenated oils, artificial sweeteners, emulsifiers, and stabilisers. These foods are often characterised by their low nutritional value and high levels of unhealthy fats, sugars, and sodium. UPF falls under the NOVA classification system's fourth category, which denotes food products that are significantly altered from their original state through processing and contain minimal whole foods. If you haven't yet explored the NOVA classification system you may wish to go online and have a look as this can be a helpful guide to understanding the processing levels within foods. Increasingly, people are opting to avoid UPF due to growing awareness of its potential adverse effects on health, including contributing to obesity, heart disease, and other chronic illnesses.

The avoidance of UPF is driven by various factors, including concerns about its impact on health and well-being. Research has shown that regular consumption of UPF is associated with an increased risk of obesity, metabolic syndrome, and various other health issues. Additionally, there is a growing recognition of the environmental implications of UPF production, including its contribution to carbon emissions, deforestation, and waste generation. As people become more health-conscious and environmentally aware, they are actively seeking alternatives to UPF, such as whole foods and minimally processed options. By choosing to avoid UPF, individuals aim to prioritise their health and support more sustainable food systems that prioritise nutrition and environmental stewardship.

Feeding Your Microbiome by Eating 30 Plants Each Week

Research is increasingly showing that incorporating a diverse range of plant-based foods into your diet, aiming for around 30 different types per week, can significantly benefit your microbiome—the community of microorganisms residing in your digestive tract. Each plant contains a unique array of fibres, phytonutrients, and other compounds that serve as nourishment for various beneficial bacteria in the gut. By consuming a wide variety of plants, you provide these microbes with a diverse range of substrates to thrive on, promoting microbial diversity and a healthier gut ecosystem. This research underscores the importance of viewing food not just as a source of energy but as a key determinant of microbial health, highlighting the profound impact that dietary choices can have on human health at the microorganism level.

Furthermore, incorporating fermented foods into the diet can complement efforts to enhance gut health. Fermented foods like sourdough, yoghurt, kefir, kimchi, sauerkraut, and kombucha contain probiotics—live beneficial bacteria that can help restore and maintain a healthy balance of gut microbiota. Probiotics from fermented foods can aid in digestion, improve immune function, and reduce inflammation in the gut, contributing to overall gut health.

What is the Deli Method?

5 salads + 5 main proteins + 4 sides per week

The deli method is a simple way of preparing fresh, whole foods to create an abundance of meal choices with minimal food processing and less effort. By choosing 5 salads, packed with different types of plants, 5 main proteins and 4 side dishes you can turn your fridge into your own home deli counter. Through the week you can then pick and choose different combos to create varied and delicious meals all week.

By following this simple structure, you can whip up dishes once or twice a week and feast all week long. We've created recipes that are super flexible depending on your own needs and all our recipes can easily be scaled up or down. The point of this book is to get your ideas flowing so you can build up your own repertoire of go-to dishes that come together to create amazing meals.

We'll also look at quick snacks you can have prepped and ready to grab and go as well as some shortcuts where we've found premade options that fit the UPF-free bill.

Salads

Tangy Thai Papaya Salad

Ingredients:

- 1 green papaya, peeled and finely sliced (firm mango or pineapple works well too)
- 1 carrot, peeled and grated
- 1 handful peanuts, chopped
- 1 handful fresh cilantro/coriander, chopped
- 1 handful fresh mint leaves, chopped
- 2 tablespoons fish sauce (optional, we like Blue Dragon or Squid brand)
- 2 tablespoons lime juice
- 1 tablespoon brown sugar
- 1 garlic clove, minced
- 1 red chilli, minced (optional)
- Salt to taste

Method:

1. In a large bowl, combine the sliced green papaya, grated carrot, chopped peanuts, chopped cilantro, and chopped mint leaves.
2. In a small bowl, whisk together the fish sauce, lime juice, brown sugar, minced garlic, minced Thai chilli (if using), and salt to make the dressing.
3. Pour the dressing over the salad and toss gently to combine.
4. Let the salad sit for at least 10 minutes to allow the flavours to develop.

Summer Berry Spinach Salad

Ingredients:

- 100g baby spinach leaves
- 1 handful mixed berries (such as strawberries, blueberries and raspberries)
- 30g sliced almonds, toasted
- 2 tablespoons balsamic vinegar ("contains sulphites" on the label is due to the fact that this is made from wine and contains an allergen, this is still a traditional food)
- Salt and pepper to taste

Method:

1. In a large bowl, combine the baby spinach leaves, mixed berries, and toasted sliced almonds.
2. Drizzle the balsamic glaze over the salad and toss gently to coat.
3. Season with salt and pepper to taste.
4. Serve immediately and revel in the summery sweetness!

Crunchy Asian Slaw

Ingredients:

- ½ head of purple cabbage, finely sliced
- 1 carrot, peeled and grated
- 1 red pepper, thinly sliced
- 1 handful chopped coriander/cilantro
- 4 chopped spring onions
- 2 tablespoons soy sauce
- 1 tablespoon sesame oil
- 1 tablespoon rice vinegar or vinegar of choice
- 1 thumb sized piece of ginger, grated (I store my ginger in the freezer and grate from frozen, no need to peel it either)
- 1 garlic clove, minced
- 1 teaspoon honey
- Salt and pepper to taste

Method:

1. In a large bowl, combine the cabbage, carrot, sliced pepper, chopped cilantro, and chopped spring onions.
2. In a small bowl, whisk together the soy sauce, sesame oil, rice vinegar, grated ginger, minced garlic, honey, salt, and pepper to make the dressing.
3. Pour the dressing over the salad and toss gently to combine.
4. Let the salad sit for at least 10 minutes to allow the flavours to meld together and served chilled.

Quinoa Power Salad

Ingredients:

- 200g quinoa, rinsed
- 1 tin black beans, drained and rinsed
- 200g corn kernels (fresh, frozen, or canned)
- 1 avocado, diced
- 1 handful cup chopped fresh coriander/cilantro or basil for coriander haters
- Juice of 2 limes
- 2 tablespoons extra virgin olive oil
- Salt and pepper to taste

Method:

1. Cook the quinoa according to package instructions and let it cool to room temperature.
2. In a large bowl, combine the cooked quinoa, black beans, corn kernels, diced avocado, and chopped cilantro.
3. In a small bowl, whisk together the lime juice, extra virgin olive oil, salt, and pepper to make the dressing.
4. Pour the dressing over the salad and toss gently to coat.
5. Serve chilled or at room temperature. You may choose to add chopped nuts and seeds if you want to pack in even more nutrition.

Caprese Salad with a Peachy Twist

Ingredients:

- 2 large peaches, sliced
- 1 ball fresh mozzarella cheese, ripped
- Handful of fresh basil leaves
- Balsamic vinegar, for drizzling
- Extra virgin olive oil, for drizzling
- Salt and pepper to taste

Method:

1. Arrange the peach slices and fresh mozzarella slices on a serving platter.
2. Tuck the fresh basil leaves between the peach and mozzarella.
3. Drizzle with balsamic and extra virgin olive oil.
4. Season with salt and pepper to taste. You may also add a drizzle of honey if you like things on the sweet side.

Roasted Vegetable Salad

Ingredients:

- 2 peppers (ideally different colours for varied nutrients), seeded and sliced
- 2 courgettes, sliced
- 2 aubergines, sliced
- 2 red onions, sliced
- 2 tablespoons extra virgin olive oil
- 2 cloves garlic, minced
- 1 teaspoon dried thyme or oregano
- Salt and pepper to taste
- Lemon for squeezing over (optional)

Method:

1. Preheat the oven to 400°F (200°C).
2. In a large bowl, toss together the sliced peppers, courgette, aubergine and red onion with the extra virgin olive oil, minced garlic, dried thyme, salt, and pepper.
3. Spread the vegetables in a single layer on a baking sheet.
4. Roast in the preheated oven for 20-25 minutes, or until the vegetables are tender and lightly caramelised, stirring halfway through.
5. Let the roasted vegetables cool slightly and squeeze over the juice of the lemon before serving.

Greek Orzo Salad

Ingredients:

- 250g orzo pasta, cooked according to package instructions and cooled
- 2 handfuls cherry tomatoes, halved
- 1/2 cucumber, diced
- 2 tbsp capers (you may use olives but I find UPF free capers easier to source)
- 200g crumbled feta cheese
- 3 tablespoons extra virgin olive oil
- 2 tablespoon red wine vinegar
- 1 teaspoon dried oregano or mixed herbs
- Salt and pepper to taste

Method:

1. In a large bowl, combine the cooked orzo pasta, halved cherry tomatoes, diced cucumber, halved Kalamata olives, and crumbled feta cheese.
2. In a small bowl, whisk together the extra virgin olive oil, red wine vinegar, dried oregano, salt, and pepper to make the dressing.
3. Pour the dressing over the salad and toss gently to combine. If you're looking for something richer, add in a tub of mascarpone and the juice of 1 lemon.

Kale, Caesar! Salad

Ingredients:

- 100g chopped kale leaves
- 1/2 cucumber, sliced (optional but lightens the salad up)
- 100g grated Parmesan cheese
- 1 handful croutons (we make ours with sourdough chunks fried in olive oil or when in a rush I use crushed Crosta & Mollica breadsticks)
- 2 tablespoons olive oil
- 1 tablespoon lemon juice
- 1 garlic clove, minced
- 1 teaspoon Dijon mustard
- Salt and pepper to taste

Method:

1. In a large bowl, massage the chopped kale leaves with olive oil and lemon juice for a few minutes to soften them.
2. Add the cucumber, grated Parmesan cheese, and croutons to the bowl.
3. In a small bowl, whisk together the minced garlic, Dijon mustard, salt, and pepper to make the dressing.
4. Pour the dressing over the salad and toss gently to combine.

Asian Style Sesame Cucumber Salad

Ingredients:

- 2 cucumbers, thinly sliced or even better chopped into quarters then placed in a bag and lightly smashed with a rolling pin
- 2 tablespoons rice vinegar or vinegar of choice (or lime juice also works well)
- 1 tablespoon soy sauce
- 1 tablespoon sesame oil
- 1 teaspoon honey
- 1 teaspoon sesame seeds (toasted in a dry pan if preferred)
- 2 spring onions, thinly sliced
- Salt and pepper to taste

Method:

1. In a large bowl, combine the cucumbers and sliced onions.
2. In a small bowl, whisk together the rice vinegar, soy sauce, sesame oil, honey, sesame seeds, salt, and pepper to make the dressing.
3. Pour the dressing over the cucumber salad and toss gently to coat.
4. Let the salad marinate for at least 15 minutes before serving to allow the flavours to meld together.

Beetroot and Goat Cheese Salad

Ingredients:

- 4 medium beetroots, roasted, peeled, and sliced (or prepacked are often UPF free)
- 100g mixed salad greens
- 80g cup crumbled goat cheese
- 80g cup chopped walnuts, toasted
- 2 tablespoons balsamic vinegar
- 1 tablespoon honey
- 1 tablespoon cup extra virgin olive oil
- Salt and pepper to taste

Method:

1. In a large bowl, combine the roasted and sliced beets, mixed salad greens, crumbled goat cheese, and toasted chopped walnuts.
2. In a small bowl, whisk together the balsamic vinegar, honey, extra virgin olive oil, salt, and pepper to make the dressing.
3. Pour the dressing over the salad and toss gently to combine.

Strawberry Spinach Salad

Ingredients:

- 100g baby spinach leaves
- 100g sliced strawberries
- 100g crumbled feta cheese
- Small handful cup sliced almonds, toasted
- 2 tablespoons balsamic vinegar
- Salt and pepper and a drizzle of honey to taste (optional)

Method:

1. In a large bowl, combine the baby spinach leaves, sliced strawberries, crumbled feta cheese, and toasted sliced almonds.
2. Drizzle the balsamic glaze over the salad and toss gently to coat.
3. Season with salt, pepper and honey to taste.

Watermelon Feta Salad

Ingredients:

- 250g cubed watermelon
- 200g crumbled feta cheese
- 1 handful cup chopped fresh mint leaves
- 2 tablespoons balsamic vinegar
- Salt, pepper and chilli to taste

Method:

1. In a large bowl, combine the cubed watermelon, crumbled feta cheese, and chopped fresh mint leaves.
2. Drizzle the balsamic glaze over the salad and toss gently to coat.
3. Season with salt, pepper and sliced chillies to taste.

Grilled Peach Salad

Ingredients:

- 2 peaches, halved and pitted
- 100g mixed salad greens
- 100g crumbled goat cheese (optional)
- 1 handful chopped pecans, toasted
- 2 tablespoons honey
- 2 tablespoons balsamic vinegar
- 2 tablespoons extra virgin olive oil
- Salt and pepper to taste

Method:

1. Preheat a grill or grill pan over medium heat.
2. Grill the peach halves for 2-3 minutes on each side, until grill marks appear.
3. Remove the grilled peaches from the grill and let them cool slightly before slicing.
4. In a large bowl, combine the mixed salad greens, sliced grilled peaches, crumbled goat cheese, and toasted chopped pecans.
5. In a small bowl, whisk together the honey, balsamic vinegar, extra virgin olive oil, salt, and pepper to make the dressing.
6. Pour the dressing over the salad and toss gently to combine.

Avocado Tomato Salad

Ingredients:

- 2 avocados, diced
- 4 salad tomatoes, diced
- 1 red onion, finely chopped
- 2 tablespoons chopped fresh coriander/cilantro
- Juice of 1 lime
- 1 tablespoon extra virgin olive oil
- Salt and pepper to taste

Method:

1. In a large bowl, combine the diced avocados, diced tomatoes, finely chopped red onion, and chopped fresh cilantro.
2. Drizzle the lime juice and extra virgin olive oil over the salad.
3. Season with salt and pepper to taste.
4. Gently toss to combine. Store in an airtight container in the fridge.

Jalapeño, Mango & Prawn Chopped Salad

Ingredients:

- 250g large prawns, peeled and deveined
- 2 ripe mangoes, diced
- 1 jalapeño pepper or similar chilli, seeded and diced
- 1 red pepper, diced
- 1/2 red onion, finely chopped
- 1 handful chopped fresh coriander/cilantro
- Juice of 2 limes
- 2 tablespoons extra virgin olive oil
- Salt and pepper to taste
- 100g mixed salad greens, for serving

Method:

1. Heat a grill or grill pan over medium-high heat.
2. Season the prawns with salt and pepper.
3. Grill the prawns for 2-3 minutes on each side, until they are pink and cooked through. Remove from heat and let cool slightly.
4. In a large bowl, combine the diced mangoes, diced jalapeño pepper, diced red bell pepper, finely chopped red onion, and chopped fresh cilantro.
5. Cut the grilled prawns into bite-sized pieces and add them to the bowl.
6. In a small bowl, whisk together the lime juice, extra virgin olive oil, salt, and pepper to make the dressing.
7. Pour the dressing over the salad and toss gently to combine.
8. Serve the salad on a bed of mixed salad greens.

Cheesy Potato & Fennel Salad

Ingredients:

- 1kg baby potatoes, halved
- 1 fennel bulb, thinly sliced
- 100g cup grated mature cheddar cheese
- 1 handful chopped fresh parsley
- 250ml creme fraiche
- ½ nutmeg, finely grated
- 1 tablespoon apple cider vinegar or vinegar of choice
- Salt and pepper to taste

Method:

1. Bring a pot of salted water to a boil. Add the baby potatoes and cook until fork-tender, about 10-12 minutes. Drain and let cool slightly.
2. In a large bowl, combine the halved baby potatoes, thinly sliced fennel bulb, shredded cheddar cheese, and chopped fresh parsley.
3. In a small bowl, whisk together the creme fraiche, vinegar, salt, and pepper to make the dressing.
4. Pour the dressing over the potato and fennel mixture and toss gently to coat. FInish with grated nutmeg.

Fresh Peach and Mozzarella Salad

Ingredients:

- 4 peaches, pitted and cut into wedges
- 100g fresh baby spinach leaves
- 2 balls mozzarella, roughly torn
- 1 handful fresh basil leaves
- 2 tablespoons honey
- 2 tablespoons balsamic vinegar
- 2 tablespoons extra virgin olive oil
- Salt and pepper to taste

Method:

1. In a small bowl whisk together the vinegar, oil and honey.
2. On a platter, scatter the spinach leaves and top with the fresh peach, mozzarella and basil leaves.
3. Drizzle the dressing over the salad when ready to serve.

Citrus and Fresh Mint Salad

Ingredients:

- 2 oranges, peeled and sliced
- 2 grapefruits, peeled and sliced
- 2 blood oranges, peeled and sliced (if available, otherwise use more regular oranges)
- Zest and juice of 1 unwaxed lime (or lemon if preferred)
- 1 handful fresh mint leaves, chopped
- 2 tablespoons honey
- 1 large handful pistachios, toasted in a dry frying pan and then chopped
- Pinch of salt

Method:

1. Arrange the sliced oranges, grapefruits, blood oranges (if using) on a serving platter. Zest the lime over the fruit.
2. Sprinkle the chopped fresh mint leaves over the citrus slices.
3. In a small bowl, whisk together the honey, lime juice and a pinch of salt.
4. Drizzle the honey mixture over the citrus slices.
5. Sprinkle the chopped pistachios over the salad for added crunch.

Courgette, Green Bean & Pepper Salad With Lemon Vinaigrette

Ingredients:

For the salad:

- 2 courgettes (zucchini), thinly sliced
- 200g green beans, trimmed and halved
- 1 red pepper, thinly sliced
- 1 yellow pepper, thinly sliced
- 1 handful chopped fresh parsley
- 1 handful chopped fresh basil

For the lemon vinaigrette:

- Juice of 2 lemons
- 3 tbsp extra virgin olive oil
- 1 garlic clove, minced
- Salt and pepper to taste

Method:

1. Bring a pot of salted water to a boil. Add the green beans and cook for 2-3 minutes, until they are crisp-tender. Drain and immediately transfer to a bowl of ice cold water to stop the cooking process. Drain again and set aside.
2. In a large mixing bowl, combine the thinly sliced courgettes, blanched green beans, thinly sliced red and yellow bell peppers, chopped fresh parsley, and chopped fresh basil.
3. In a small bowl, whisk together the lemon juice, extra virgin olive oil, minced garlic, salt, and pepper to make the vinaigrette.
4. Pour the lemon vinaigrette over the salad ingredients and toss gently to coat.
5. Let the salad marinate for at least 15 minutes to allow the flavours to meld together.

Tuna & Green Bean Chopped Salad

Ingredients:

- 200g green beans, trimmed and halved
- 2 small cans tuna in water, drained
- 150g cherry tomatoes, halved
- 1/2 red onion, thinly sliced
- 1 handful chopped fresh parsley
- 1 handful cup chopped fresh basil
- 2 tablespoons capers, drained
- 2 tablespoons extra virgin olive oil
- 1 tablespoon red wine vinegar
- 1 teaspoon miso paste (optional, adds a great umami richness)
- Salt and pepper to taste
- Lemon wedges, for serving

Method:

1. Bring a pot of salted water to a boil. Add the green beans and cook for 2-3 minutes, until they are crisp-tender. Drain and immediately transfer to a bowl of ice water to stop the cooking process. Drain again and set aside.
2. In a large mixing bowl, combine the blanched green beans, drained tuna, halved cherry tomatoes, thinly sliced red onion, chopped fresh parsley, chopped fresh basil, and drained capers.
3. In a small bowl, whisk together the extra virgin olive oil, red wine vinegar, miso (if using) plus salt, and pepper to make the dressing.
4. Pour the dressing over the salad ingredients and toss gently to coat.
5. Serve the Tuna & Green Bean Chopped Salad chilled or at room temperature, with lemon wedges on the side for squeezing over the salad.

Carrot & Almond Rice Salad With Mint Yoghurt

Ingredients:

For the salad:

- 300g cooked rice (preferably basmati or jasmine)
- 2 large carrots, grated
- 1 handful sliced almonds, toasted
- 1 handful dried cranberries or raisins
- 1 handful cup chopped fresh cilantro (coriander)

For the mint yoghurt dressing:

- 100g cup natural Greek yoghurt (avoid "Greek style" yoghurt where possible)
- 2 tablespoons fresh mint leaves, finely chopped
- 1 tablespoon lemon juice
- 1 tablespoon honey
- Salt and pepper to taste

Method:

1. In a large mixing bowl, combine the cooked rice, grated carrots, sliced almonds, dried cranberries or raisins, and chopped fresh coriander.
2. In a small bowl, whisk together the Greek yoghurt, finely chopped fresh mint leaves, lemon juice, honey, salt, and pepper to make the dressing.
3. Pour the mint yoghurt dressing over the salad ingredients and toss gently to coat.

Warm Caprese Butter Bean Salad

Ingredients:

- 2 x 400g tins butter beans, drained and rinsed
- 150g cherry tomatoes, halved
- 1 ball fresh mozzarella cheese, torn gently
- 1 handful chopped fresh basil
- 2 tablespoons balsamic vinegar
- 2 tablespoons extra virgin olive oil
- Salt and pepper to taste

Method:

1. In a large skillet, heat the extra virgin olive oil over medium heat.
2. Add the drained and rinsed butter beans to the skillet. Cook for 3-4 minutes, stirring occasionally, until heated through.
3. Add the halved cherry tomatoes to the skillet with the butter beans. Cook for an additional 2-3 minutes, until the tomatoes are slightly softened.
4. Remove the skillet from the heat and stir in the diced fresh mozzarella cheese and chopped fresh basil.
5. Drizzle the balsamic vinegar over the salad and toss gently to combine.
6. Season with salt and pepper to taste.

Fregola Salad with Roasted Peppers and Red Onion

Ingredients:

- 200g fregola (giant couscous but regular works too)
- 2 red peppers
- ½ tsp cumin seeds
- 1 red onion, thinly sliced
- 2 tablespoons extra virgin olive oil plus extra for roasting the peppers
- 2 tablespoons balsamic vinegar
- 1 handful chopped fresh parsley
- Salt and pepper to taste

Method:

1. Preheat the oven to 400°F (200°C).
2. Place the red peppers on a baking sheet. Drizzle with olive oil and sprinkle with cumin seeds. Roast in the preheated oven for 20-25 minutes, or until the peppers are softened. Remove from the oven and let cool slightly.
3. Once the peppers are cool enough to handle, peel off the skin, remove the seeds, and slice them into strips. Dunking in ice water helps make this easier and it is entirely optional, I sometimes leave the skin for added fibre.
4. In a large pot of salted boiling water, cook the fregola according to package instructions until al dente. Drain and rinse under cold water to stop the cooking process. Let cool.
5. In a pan, heat 1 tablespoon of olive oil over medium heat. Add the thinly sliced red onion and sauté for 5-7 minutes, until softened and slightly caramelised. Remove from heat and let cool.
6. In a large mixing bowl, combine the cooked fregola, roasted red pepper strips, sautéed red onion, chopped fresh parsley, remaining olive oil, and balsamic vinegar. Toss gently to combine.

7. Season with salt and pepper to taste.

Grapefruit Rice Noodle Salad

Ingredients:

For the salad:

- 200g rice noodles
- 1 grapefruit, segmented
- 1 cucumber, julienned
- 1 carrot, julienned
- 1 handful chopped fresh cilantro/coriander (or parsley for coriander haters)
- 1 handful chopped fresh mint
- 3 tbsp chopped roasted peanuts

For the dressing:

- Juice of 1 lime
- 2 tablespoons soy sauce
- 1 tablespoon honey
- 1 tablespoon sesame oil
- 1 teaspoon grated ginger
- 1 garlic clove, minced
- Red chilli flakes or fresh slices to taste (optional)

Method:

1. Cook the rice noodles according to the package instructions. Drain and rinse under cold water to stop the cooking process. Set aside.
2. In a large mixing bowl, combine the cooked rice noodles, segmented grapefruit, julienned cucumber, julienned carrot, chopped fresh cilantro, chopped fresh mint, and chopped roasted peanuts.
3. In a small bowl, whisk together the lime juice, soy sauce, honey, sesame oil, grated ginger, minced garlic, and red chilli (if using) to make the dressing.

4. Pour the dressing over the salad ingredients and toss gently to coat.

Charred Broccoli & Crispy Chickpea Salad

Ingredients:

For the salad:

- 1 head of broccoli, cut into florets
- 1 can chickpeas, drained, rinsed, and patted dry
- 2 tablespoons olive oil
- Salt and pepper to taste

- 100g mixed salad greens
- 100g cup crumbled feta cheese (optional)
- 2 tablespoons chopped fresh parsley (for garnish)

For the dressing:

- 2 tablespoons tahini
- 2 tablespoons lemon juice
- 1 tablespoon water
- 1 garlic clove, minced
- Salt and pepper to taste

Method:

1. Preheat the oven to 400°F (200°C).
2. Place the chickpeas on a baking sheet lined with parchment paper. Drizzle with 1 tablespoon of olive oil and season with salt and pepper. Toss to coat evenly. Roast in the preheated oven for 20-25 minutes, or until crispy and golden brown.
3. In a large mixing bowl, toss the broccoli florets with the remaining tablespoon of olive oil, salt, and pepper. Spread them out on a baking sheet in a single layer. Roast in the preheated oven for 15-20 minutes, or until charred and tender.
4. In a small bowl, whisk together the tahini, lemon juice, water, minced garlic, salt, and pepper to make the dressing. Adjust the consistency with more water if needed.
5. In a large serving bowl, arrange the mixed salad greens. Top with the roasted broccoli florets and crispy chickpeas.
6. Drizzle the tahini dressing over the salad.
7. If desired, sprinkle crumbled feta cheese over the top.
8. Garnish with chopped fresh parsley.

Avocado, Kale & Feta Salad

Ingredients:

- 200g kale leaves, stems removed and torn into bite-sized pieces (or ready chopped)
- 2 ripe avocados, diced
- 100g cup crumbled feta cheese
- 1 handful sliced almonds, toasted
- 2 tablespoons dried cranberries or raisins (some do have sunflower oil in them but I feel this isn't too terrible in the grand scheme of things but shop around if this is important to you or omit altogether)
- 2 tablespoons lemon juice
- 2 tablespoons extra virgin olive oil
- 1 teaspoon honey
- Salt and pepper to taste

Method:

1. In a small bowl, whisk together the lemon juice, extra virgin olive oil, honey, salt, and pepper to make the dressing.
2. Pour the dressing over the kale and using clean hands, massage the dressing into the kale leaves for 1-2 minutes. This helps to tenderise the kale and infuse it with flavour.
3. In a large mixing bowl, combine the kale leaves, diced avocado, crumbled feta cheese, toasted sliced almonds, and dried cranberries or raisins before serving.

Tomato and Ginger Salad

Ingredients:

- 4 large tomatoes, sliced
- 1-inch piece of ginger, grated (I prefer to do this from frozen and I leave the skin on, if using fresh you may choose to peel the ginger by using the edge of a teaspoon to take off the thin skin)
- 2 tablespoons chopped fresh cilantro (coriander)
- 1 tablespoon rice vinegar or vinegar of choice
- 1 tablespoon soy sauce
- 1 tablespoon sesame oil
- 1 teaspoon honey
- Salt and pepper to taste
- Sesame seeds for garnish (optional)

Method:

1. Arrange the sliced tomatoes on a serving platter.
2. In a small bowl, combine the grated ginger, chopped fresh cilantro, rice vinegar, soy sauce, sesame oil, honey, salt, and pepper to make the dressing.
3. Drizzle the dressing over the sliced tomatoes.
4. Garnish with sesame seeds if desired.

Aubergine Parmigiana Salad

Ingredients:

For the grilled aubergine:

- 2 large aubergines (eggplants), sliced into rounds
- 2 tablespoons olive oil
- Salt and pepper to taste

For the salad:

- 100g mixed salad leaves
- 100g cherry tomatoes, halved
- 1 handful cup chopped fresh basil
- 50g grated Parmesan cheese

For the balsamic glaze:

- 2 tbsp balsamic vinegar
- 1 tablespoon honey

Method:

1. Preheat the grill or grill pan over medium-high heat.
2. Brush the sliced aubergine rounds with olive oil and season with salt and pepper.
3. Grill the aubergine rounds for 3-4 minutes on each side, until tender and grill marks appear. Remove from heat and let cool slightly.
4. In a large mixing bowl, combine the mixed salad greens, halved cherry tomatoes, chopped fresh basil, and grated Parmesan cheese.
5. Arrange the grilled aubergine rounds on top of the salad.
6. In a small saucepan, heat the balsamic vinegar and honey over medium heat. Simmer for 3-4 minutes, stirring occasionally, until the mixture has thickened slightly.

7. Drizzle the balsamic glaze over the salad.

Nectarine & Burrata Salad With Charred Lemon Dressing

Ingredients:

For the salad:

- 2 ripe nectarines, thinly sliced
- 1 ball burrata cheese
- 100g rocket leaves
- 1 handful toasted walnuts, chopped
- 1 tablespoon fresh basil leaves, torn

- Salt and black pepper to taste

For the charred lemon dressing:

- 1 lemon, halved
- 3 tablespoons extra virgin olive oil
- 1 teaspoon honey
- Salt and black pepper to taste

Method:

1. Preheat a grill pan or frying pan over medium-high heat.
2. Place the lemon halves cut-side down on the pan. Grill for 3-4 minutes until charred. Remove and let cool.
3. In a small bowl, squeeze the juice from the charred lemon halves. Add extra virgin olive oil, honey, salt, and black pepper to taste. Whisk until well combined to make the dressing.
4. In a large serving platter, arrange the rocket.
5. Scatter the thinly sliced nectarines over the rocket.
6. Tear the burrata cheese into pieces (be careful, this may get messy) and place on top of the salad.
7. Sprinkle with toasted walnuts and torn basil leaves.
8. Drizzle the charred lemon dressing over the salad.
9. Season with salt and black pepper to taste.

Tomato & Mint Salad With Spicy Paprika Vinaigrette

Ingredients:

For the salad:

- 6 large tomatoes, sliced
- 1 handful cup fresh mint leaves, chopped
- 1/2 red onion, thinly sliced
- 100g crumbled feta cheese (optional)
- Salt and black pepper to taste

For the spicy paprika vinaigrette:

- 2 tablespoons extra virgin olive oil
- 1 tablespoon red wine vinegar
- 1 teaspoon honey
- 1 teaspoon smoked paprika
- 1/4 teaspoon chilli powder
- 1/4 teaspoon cayenne pepper (optional, adjust to taste)
- Salt and black pepper to taste

Method:

1. Arrange the sliced tomatoes on a serving platter.
2. Sprinkle chopped fresh mint leaves and thinly sliced red onion over the tomatoes.
3. If using, scatter crumbled feta cheese on top of the salad.
4. In a small bowl, whisk together extra virgin olive oil, red wine vinegar, honey, paprika, chilli powder, cayenne pepper, salt, and black pepper to make the spicy paprika vinaigrette.
5. Drizzle the vinaigrette over and season with additional salt and black pepper if needed.

Pear & Chicory Salad

Ingredients:

For the salad:

- 2 heads chicory, leaves separated
- 4 pears, thinly sliced
- 1 handful cup walnuts, toasted and chopped
- 75g crumbled blue cheese
- Salt and black pepper to taste

For the dressing:

- 3 tablespoons extra virgin olive oil
- 2 tablespoons apple cider vinegar
- 1 tablespoon honey
- Salt and black pepper to taste

Method:

1. Arrange the chicory leaves on a serving platter.
2. Scatter thinly sliced pears and toasted chopped walnuts over the chicory leaves.
3. If using, sprinkle crumbled blue cheese over the salad.
4. In a small bowl, whisk together extra virgin olive oil, apple cider vinegar, honey, salt, and black pepper to make the dressing.
5. Drizzle the dressing over just before serving and season with additional salt and black pepper if needed.

Halloumi & Pomegranate Salad

Ingredients:

- 225g halloumi cheese, sliced
- 100g mixed salad greens
- Seeds from 1 pomegranate
- 1 handful chopped fresh mint leaves
- 2 tablespoons extra virgin olive oil
- 1 tablespoon balsamic vinegar
- 1 teaspoon honey
- Salt and black pepper to taste

Method:

1. Heat a grill pan or skillet over medium-high heat.
2. Place the halloumi slices in the pan and cook for 2-3 minutes on each side, or until golden brown and crispy.
3. In a large mixing bowl, combine the mixed salad greens, pomegranate and chopped fresh mint leaves.
4. In a small bowl, whisk together the extra virgin olive oil, balsamic vinegar, honey, salt, and black pepper to make the dressing.
5. Drizzle the dressing over the salad ingredients and toss gently to coat.
6. Divide the salad onto serving plates and top with the grilled halloumi slices.

Burrata & Shaved Cucumber Salad With Green Chilli Oil

Ingredients:

For the salad:

- 1 ball burrata cheese
- 2 cucumbers, thinly shaved
- 1 handful fresh basil leaves
- 1 handful fresh mint leaves
- Salt and black pepper to taste

For the green chilli oil:

- 2 green chillies, thinly sliced
- 4 tbsp extra virgin olive oil
- 1 garlic clove, minced
- Zest of 1 lemon
- Salt to taste

Method:

1. In a small saucepan, heat the extra virgin olive oil over low heat. Add the sliced green chillies and minced garlic. Cook gently for 3-4 minutes, or until the garlic is fragrant and the chillies are softened.
2. Remove the saucepan from the heat and stir in the lemon zest and salt. Set aside to cool.
3. Arrange the thinly shaved cucumbers on a serving platter.
4. Tear the burrata cheese into gorgeous gooey pieces and place on top of the cucumbers.
5. Scatter fresh basil and mint leaves over the salad.
6. Drizzle the green chilli oil over the salad just before serving.
7. Season with salt and black pepper to taste.

Sticky Honey Roasted Carrots on Puy Lentil Salad

Ingredients:

For the sticky honey roasted carrots:

- 5 large carrots, peeled and cut lengthwise
- 2 tablespoons olive oil
- 2 tablespoons honey
- 1 tablespoon balsamic vinegar
- Salt and black pepper to taste

For the Puy lentil salad:

- 200g Puy lentils
- 400ml water
- 1 red onion, finely diced
- 2 cloves garlic, minced
- 2 tablespoons extra virgin olive oil
- 2 tablespoons balsamic vinegar
- Salt and black pepper to taste
- 1 handful chopped fresh parsley
- 100g crumbled feta cheese (optional)

Method:

1. Preheat the oven to 400°F (200°C).
2. In a mixing bowl, combine the carrots with olive oil, honey, balsamic vinegar, salt, and black pepper. Toss until the carrots are evenly coated.
3. Arrange the coated carrots on a baking sheet lined with parchment paper. Roast in the preheated oven for 20-25 minutes, or until the carrots are tender and caramelised.
4. While the carrots are roasting, rinse the lentils under cold water. In a saucepan, bring the water to a boil. Add the rinsed lentils and reduce the heat to low. Simmer for 20-25 minutes, or until the lentils are tender but still hold their

shape. Drain any excess liquid and set aside.

5. In a skillet, heat extra virgin olive oil over medium heat. Add the finely diced red onion and minced garlic. Sauté for 5-7 minutes, or until the onions are soft and translucent.
6. In a large mixing bowl, combine the cooked lentils with the sautéed onions and garlic. Drizzle with balsamic vinegar, and season with salt and black pepper to taste. Toss to combine.
7. Arrange the salad on a serving platter. Top with the sticky honey roasted carrots.
8. Garnish with chopped fresh parsley and crumbled feta cheese, if desired.

Shredded Brussels Sprout Salad with Pomegranate and Yoghurt Dressing

Ingredients:

For the salad:

- 300g Brussels sprouts, trimmed and thinly shredded
- Seeds from 1 pomegranate
- 1 handful cup toasted almonds, chopped
- 2 tablespoons chopped fresh mint leaves
- 2 tablespoons chopped fresh parsley leaves

For the yoghurt dressing:

- 100g Greek yoghurt (avoid "Greek style" yoghurt where possible)
- 2 tablespoons lemon juice
- 1 tablespoon honey
- 1 tablespoon extra virgin olive oil
- Salt and black pepper to taste

Method:

1. In a large mixing bowl, combine the shredded Brussels sprouts, pomegranate arils, chopped toasted almonds, chopped fresh mint leaves, and chopped fresh parsley leaves.
2. In a separate small bowl, whisk together the Greek yoghurt, lemon juice, honey, extra virgin olive oil, salt, and black pepper to make the dressing.
3. Pour the yoghurt dressing over the salad ingredients.
4. Toss gently until all the ingredients are evenly coated with the dressing.
5. Taste and adjust seasoning if needed, adding more salt and black pepper if desired.

Radicchio and Fresh Gremolata Salad

Ingredients:

For the salad:

- 1 head radicchio, thinly sliced
- 1 handful pine nuts, toasted
- 80g shaved Parmesan cheese

For the gremolata:

- 1 handful chopped fresh parsley
- Zest of 1 lemon
- 2 cloves garlic, minced
- 2 tablespoons extra virgin olive oil

Method:

1. In a large mixing bowl, combine the thinly sliced radicchio, toasted pine nuts, and shaved Parmesan cheese.
2. In a separate small bowl, mix together the chopped fresh parsley, lemon zest, minced garlic, and extra virgin olive oil to make the gremolata.
3. Drizzle the gremolata over the salad ingredients.
4. Toss gently until all the ingredients are evenly coated with the gremolata.

Wedge Salad with Blue Cheese Dressing

Ingredients:

For the salad:

- 1 head iceberg lettuce, cut into wedges
- 100g sugar snap peas, halved lengthwise to expose the peas
- 1 handful chopped chives (for garnish)
- Salt and black pepper to taste

For the blue cheese dressing:

- 100ml sour cream
- 100g crumbled blue cheese such as stilton
- 1 tablespoon lemon juice
- 1 clove garlic, minced
- Salt and black pepper to taste

Method:

1. Arrange the iceberg lettuce wedges on serving plates.
2. Scatter halved peas over the lettuce wedges.
3. In a small bowl, whisk together sour cream, crumbled blue cheese, lemon juice, minced garlic, salt, and black pepper to make the blue cheese dressing.
4. Drizzle the blue cheese dressing over the salad.
5. Garnish with chopped chives.
6. Season with additional salt and black pepper if desired.

Charred Corn Salad

Ingredients:

- 4 ears of corn, husked
- 1 red pepper, diced
- ½ red onion, finely chopped
- 1 jalapeño or other chilli pepper, seeded and minced
- 1 handful chopped fresh basil
- Juice of 2 limes
- 2 tablespoons extra virgin olive oil
- 1 teaspoon honey
- Salt and black pepper to taste

Method:

1. Preheat a grill or grill pan over medium-high heat.
2. Place the ears of corn on the grill and cook, turning occasionally, until charred in spots, about 8-10 minutes.
3. Remove the corn from the grill and let it cool slightly. Once cooled, cut the kernels off the cob and transfer them to a large mixing bowl.
4. Add diced red bell pepper, finely chopped red onion, minced jalapeño pepper, and chopped fresh basil to the bowl with the corn.
5. In a small bowl, whisk together lime juice, extra virgin olive oil, honey, salt, and black pepper to make the dressing.
6. Pour the dressing over the corn salad ingredients.
7. Toss gently to combine and coat everything evenly with the dressing.

Cauliflower and Tahini Verde Salad

Ingredients:

- 1 large cauliflower, cut into florets
- 2 tbsp olive oil
- Salt and black pepper to taste
- 1 large bunch of fresh parsley
- 1 large bunch of fresh coriander
- 1 garlic clove, minced
- 2 tbsp tahini
- Juice of 1 lemon
- Juice of 1 lime
- 1 tsp honey
- 2 tbsp water (or more as needed)
- 100g fresh baby spinach leaves
- 2 tbsp toasted sesame seeds

Instructions:

1. Preheat your oven to 200°C (400°F). Toss the cauliflower florets with olive oil, salt, and pepper. Spread them out on a baking tray and roast for 25-30 minutes, or until golden and tender, turning halfway through.
2. While the cauliflower is roasting, blend the parsley, coriander, garlic, tahini, lemon juice, lime juice, honey, and water until smooth. Adjust the consistency with more water if needed. Season with salt to taste.
3. Once the cauliflower is roasted, let it cool slightly. Transfer it to a large bowl and pour the green tahini dressing over the roasted cauliflower and toss to coat evenly.
4. Transfer the salad to a serving dish that has been scattered with fresh spinach leaves, and sprinkle with toasted sesame seeds.

Pearl Barley Super Salad

Ingredients:

- 200g pearl barley
- 400ml water
- 1 cup cherry tomatoes, halved
- 1 cucumber, diced
- 1 head of broccoli, finely chopped
- 1 pepper (any colour), diced

- ½ red onion, finely chopped
- 1 handful cup fresh parsley, chopped
- 1 handful fresh mint leaves, chopped
- 1 handful toasted pine nuts
- Juice of 1 lemon
- 2 tablespoons extra virgin olive oil
- Mixed seeds for topping (optional)

Method:

1. Rinse the pearl barley under cold water. In a saucepan, bring 2 cups of water or vegetable broth to a boil. Add the rinsed pearl barley, reduce heat to low, cover, and simmer for 25-30 minutes, or until the barley is tender and the liquid is absorbed. 5 minutes before the barley is ready, add in the broccoli and cover for remaining time. Remove from heat and let it cool slightly.
2. In a large mixing bowl, combine the cooked pearl barley and broccoli with cherry tomatoes, diced cucumber, diced bell pepper, finely chopped red onion, chopped fresh parsley, chopped fresh mint leaves, and toasted pine nuts.
3. In a small bowl, whisk together lemon juice, extra virgin olive oil, salt, and black pepper to make the dressing.
4. Pour the dressing over the pearl barley salad ingredients.
5. Toss gently to combine and coat everything evenly with the dressing.
6. Taste and adjust seasoning if needed, adding more salt and black pepper if desired. Top with mixed seeds if using for added fibre.

Hearty Side Dishes

Roast Sweet Potato Salad with Miso Tahini Chickpeas

Ingredients:

- 2 large sweet potatoes, peeled and diced
- 1 can chickpeas, drained and rinsed
- 2 tablespoons miso paste (we like Yutaka brand)
- 2 tablespoons tahini
- 1 tablespoon olive oil
- 1 teaspoon smoked paprika
- Salt and pepper to taste
- Mixed salad greens
- 1 handful chopped fresh coriander/cilantro (optional)
- 5 sliced spring onions
- Sesame seeds, for garnish (optional)

Method:

1. Preheat the oven to 400°F (200°C).
2. Place the diced sweet potatoes on a baking sheet lined with parchment paper. Drizzle with olive oil and sprinkle with

smoked paprika, salt, and pepper. Toss to coat evenly.

3. Roast the sweet potatoes in the preheated oven for 20-25 minutes, or until tender and golden brown.
4. In a small bowl, whisk together the miso paste, tahini, and a splash of water to thin out the mixture.
5. In a separate bowl, toss the drained and rinsed chickpeas with the miso tahini mixture until evenly coated.
6. Heat a frying pan over medium heat. Add the chickpeas and cook for 5-7 minutes, stirring occasionally, until they are lightly browned and crispy.
7. In a large bowl, combine the roasted sweet potatoes, crispy miso tahini chickpeas, mixed salad greens, chopped fresh coriander, and sliced spring onions.
8. Toss gently to combine and garnish with sesame seeds.

Baby Potatoes With Harissa Butter & Chives

Ingredients:

- 750g baby potatoes, halved
- 2 tablespoons easy harissa paste (we use 1 tbsp harissa spice mix and mix with 1 tbsp olive oil)
- 2 tablespoons unsalted butter, melted
- Salt and pepper to taste
- 1 small handful cup chopped fresh chives
- Lemon wedges, for serving

Method:

1. Bring a pot of salted water to a boil. Add the halved baby potatoes and cook until fork-tender, about 10-12 minutes. Drain and let cool slightly.
2. In a small bowl, mix together the harissa paste and melted unsalted butter.
3. Place the cooked baby potatoes in a large bowl and pour the harissa butter mixture over them. Toss gently to coat evenly.
4. Season with salt and pepper to taste.
5. Garnish with chopped fresh chives.
6. Serve the potatoes with lemon wedges on the side for squeezing over.

Crispy Rice & Smashed Cucumbers

Ingredients:

For the crispy rice:

- 1 cup cooked rice (preferably short-grain)
- 1 tablespoon sesame oil
- Salt to taste

For the smashed cucumber:

- 2 medium cucumbers
- 2 cloves garlic, minced
- 2 tablespoons rice vinegar or vinegar of choice
- 1 tablespoon soy sauce
- 1 teaspoon honey
- 1 teaspoon sesame seeds

For the salad:

- Mixed salad greens
- 1 handful chopped fresh coriander/cilantro (optional)
- 1 handful chopped green onions
- Lime wedges, for serving

Method:

1. Preheat the oven to 375°F (190°C).
2. Spread the cooked rice evenly on a baking sheet lined with parchment paper. Drizzle with sesame oil and sprinkle with salt.
3. Bake the rice in the preheated oven for 20-25 minutes, stirring occasionally, until crispy and golden brown. Remove from the oven and let cool.
4. Meanwhile, prepare the smashed cucumber. Place the cucumbers on a cutting board and gently smash them with

a rolling pin or the back of a knife. Cut them into bite-sized pieces and place them in a bowl.

5. In a small bowl, mix together the minced garlic, rice vinegar, soy sauce, honey, and sesame seeds. Pour the dressing over the smashed cucumbers and toss to coat. Let marinate for at least 10 minutes.
6. In a large bowl, combine the crispy rice, marinated smashed cucumbers, mixed salad greens, chopped fresh cilantro, and chopped green onions. Toss gently to combine.
7. Serve with lime wedges on the side for squeezing over.

Ginger and Garlic New Potatoes

Ingredients:

- 500g new potatoes, scrubbed and halved
- 2 tablespoons olive oil
- 2 cloves garlic, minced
- 1-inch piece ginger, grated
- 2 tablespoons chopped fresh parsley
- Salt and black pepper to taste
- Juice of 1 lemon
- 1 tablespoon honey
- 1 tablespoon whole grain mustard
- 2 tablespoons Greek yoghurt (avoid "Greek style" yoghurt where possible)
- 1 tablespoon chopped chives, optional for garnish

Method:

1. Place the halved new potatoes in a pot of salted water. Bring to a boil, then reduce heat and simmer for 10-12 minutes, or until potatoes are fork-tender. Drain and set aside.
2. In a skillet, heat olive oil over medium heat. Add minced garlic and grated ginger, and sauté for 1-2 minutes until fragrant.
3. Add the cooked new potatoes to the skillet with the garlic and ginger. Stir to coat the potatoes in the mixture. Cook for another 2-3 minutes to allow the flavours to meld.
4. In a small bowl, whisk together lemon juice, honey, whole grain mustard, Greek yoghurt, chopped fresh parsley, salt, and black pepper to make the dressing.
5. Pour the dressing over the warm potato mixture and toss gently to coat.
6. Transfer the potato salad to a serving bowl and garnish with chopped chives.

Roasted Squash with Chickpeas and Fennel

Ingredients:

For the salad:

- 2 large butternut squash, peeled, seeded, and cubed
- 1 fennel bulb, thinly sliced
- 1 can chickpeas, drained and rinsed
- 2 tablespoons olive oil
- 1 teaspoon ground cumin
- 1 teaspoon smoked paprika
- Salt and black pepper to taste
- 1/4 cup crumbled feta cheese (optional)
- 2 tablespoons chopped fresh parsley (for garnish)

For the dressing:

- 3 tablespoons extra virgin olive oil
- 2 tablespoons balsamic vinegar
- 1 tablespoon honey
- Salt and black pepper to taste

Method:

1. Preheat the oven to 400°F (200°C).
2. In a large mixing bowl, combine the cubed butternut squash, thinly sliced fennel, and drained chickpeas.
3. Drizzle olive oil over the vegetables and chickpeas. Sprinkle ground cumin, smoked paprika, salt, and black pepper. Toss until everything is well coated.
4. Spread the mixture out on a baking sheet in a single layer. Roast in the preheated oven for 25-30 minutes, or until the squash is tender and caramelised.
5. While the vegetables and chickpeas are roasting, prepare the dressing. In a small bowl, whisk together extra virgin olive oil, balsamic vinegar, honey, salt and black pepper.

6. Once the roasted vegetables and chickpeas are done, remove them from the oven and let them cool slightly.
7. In a large serving bowl, sprinkle crumbled feta cheese over the roasted squash, fennel and chickpeas.
8. Drizzle the dressing over and garnish with chopped fresh parsley.

Basic but Beautiful Pasta Side Dish

Ingredients:

- 400g fusilli pasta
- 100g cherry tomatoes, halved
- 1/2 cucumber, diced
- 3 tbsp capers
- ½ red onion, diced
- 1 handful chopped fresh basil
- 1 handful chopped fresh parsley
- 100g grated Parmesan cheese
- 3 tablespoons extra virgin olive oil
- 2 tablespoons red wine vinegar
- 1 teaspoon dried oregano
- Salt and black pepper to taste

Method:

1. Cook the fusilli pasta according to package instructions. Drain and rinse under cold water.
2. In a large mixing bowl, combine the cooked pasta, cherry tomatoes, diced cucumber, capers, diced red onion, chopped fresh herbs and grated parmesan cheese.
3. In a small bowl, whisk together extra virgin olive oil, red wine vinegar, dried oregano, salt, and black pepper to make the dressing.
4. Pour the dressing over the pasta salad ingredients.
5. Toss gently to combine and coat everything evenly with the dressing.
6. Taste and adjust seasoning if needed, adding more salt and black pepper if desired.

Lemon Ricotta Orzo Pasta

Ingredients:

- 200g orzo pasta
- 100g cherry tomatoes, halved
- 1 cucumber, diced
- 2 tbsp capers
- 100g crumbled feta cheese
- 100g ricotta cheese
- Juice and zest of 1 lemon
- 2 tablespoons chopped fresh parsley
- 2 tablespoons chopped fresh dill
- 3 tablespoons extra virgin olive oil
- 2 tablespoons red wine vinegar
- 1 teaspoon dried oregano
- Salt and black pepper to taste

Method:

1. Cook the orzo pasta according to package instructions. Drain and rinse under cold water.
2. In a large mixing bowl, combine the cooked orzo pasta, cherry tomatoes, diced cucumber, capers, crumbled feta cheese, chopped fresh parsley, and chopped fresh dill.
3. In a small bowl, whisk together extra virgin olive oil, red wine vinegar, dried oregano, ricotta, lemon, salt and black pepper to make the dressing. Loosen with water if too thick.
4. Pour the dressing over the pasta salad ingredients.
5. Toss gently to combine and coat everything evenly with the dressing.

Nettle Pesto Pasta

Ingredients:

- 500g cooked pasta, any shape you like (we like rigatoni for this)
- 1 small bowl of fresh stinging nettles (or Kale or spinach also works). Collect the nettles wearing gloves and then add to boiling water and cook for 5 minutes, then drain. The nettles lose all sting upon cooking. Reserve 100ml of cooking liquid in case needed later.
- 150g grated parmesan cheese
- 4 tablespoons extra virgin olive oil
- 3 cloves garlic, minced
- Toasted nuts such as pine or walnuts (optional)
- Handful of fresh basil (optional)
- Juice and zest of 1 lemon
- Salt and black pepper to taste

Method:

1. In a pestle and mortar or blender, combine the nettles, garlic, lemon, olive oil, parmesan and nuts. Bash or blend until quite smooth. Add in some reserved cooking liquid one teaspoon at a time if too thick (this will depend a lot on how young or old the nettles were).
2. If adding basil, do this now and bash or blend a little more (adding the basil last keeps it tasting fresher).
3. Pour the pesto mixture over the pasta salad ingredients.
4. Toss gently to combine and coat everything evenly with the pesto dressing.
5. Taste and adjust seasoning if needed, adding more salt and black pepper if desired. If the nettles were older, you may wish to also add in a splash more lemon juice or vinegar to break through the heavier flavour.

Southwest US Style Pasta Salad

Ingredients:

- 400g macaroni pasta, cooked
- 400g tin sweetcorn or cooked fresh/frozen corn
- 1 cup black beans, cooked
- 1 diced red pepper
- ½ red onion, diced
- 1 handful chopped fresh cilantro/coriander
- 100g grated cheddar cheese
- Zest and juice of 1 lime (if waxed just use juice)
- 2 tablespoons extra virgin olive oil
- 1 teaspoon chilli powder or chopped fresh chilli
- ½ teaspoon ground cumin
- Salt and black pepper to taste

Method:

1. In a large mixing bowl, combine the cooked pasta, corn, cooked black beans, diced red pepper, red onion, chopped fresh coriander, and cheese.
2. In a small bowl, whisk together lime juice, extra virgin olive oil, chilli powder, ground cumin, salt, and black pepper to make the dressing.
3. Pour the dressing over the pasta salad ingredients.
4. Toss gently to combine and coat everything evenly with the dressing.
5. Taste and adjust seasoning if needed, adding more salt and black pepper if desired.

Asian Style Sesame Noodle Salad

Ingredients:

- 400g rice noodles
- 1/3 red cabbage, shredded
- 2 large carrots, grated
- 1 thinly sliced red pepper
- 5 chopped spring onions
- 1 handful of sugar snap peas, thinly sliced
- 1 handful chopped coriander/cilantro (or mint for coriander haters)
- 2 tablespoons toasted sesame seeds
- 3 tablespoons soy sauce
- 2 tablespoons sesame oil
- 2 tablespoons rice vinegar or vinegar of choice
- 1 tablespoon honey
- 1 tablespoon grated fresh ginger
- 2 cloves garlic, minced
- 1 tablespoon tahini (adds a richness to the flavour), optional
- Red chilli, chopped, to taste (optional)

Method:

1. Cook noodles according to package instructions. Drain and rinse under cold water.
2. In a large mixing bowl, combine the cooked noodles, shredded cabbage, carrots, peas, pepper, onions, chopped herbs, and toasted sesame seeds.
3. In a small bowl, whisk together soy sauce, sesame oil, rice vinegar, honey, grated fresh ginger, minced garlic, and red chilli and tahini if using.
4. Pour the dressing over the noodle salad ingredients.
5. Toss gently to combine and coat everything evenly with the dressing.

6. Taste and adjust seasoning if needed.

Simple Herb Roasted Potatoes

Ingredients:

- 500g baby potatoes, halved
- 2 tablespoons olive oil
- 2 cloves garlic, minced
- 1 tablespoon chopped fresh rosemary
- 1 tablespoon chopped fresh thyme
- Salt and black pepper to taste

Method:

1. Preheat the oven to 400°F (200°C).
2. In a large bowl, toss the halved baby potatoes with olive oil, minced garlic, chopped fresh rosemary, chopped fresh thyme, salt, and black pepper until evenly coated.
3. Spread the potatoes in a single layer on a baking sheet.
4. Roast in the preheated oven for 25-30 minutes, or until golden brown and crispy.

Most Amazing Sour Cream Mashed Potatoes with Garlic and Chives

Ingredients:

- 750g large white potatoes, peeled and cubed
- 4 cloves garlic, whole
- 100ml sour cream
- 2 tablespoons butter
- 2 tablespoons chopped fresh chives
- Salt and black pepper to taste

Method:

1. Place the potatoes and peeled garlic cloves in a large pot of salted water.
2. Bring the water to a boil and cook the potatoes until fork-tender, about 15-20 minutes.
3. Drain the potatoes and garlic, then return them to the pot. Check your garlic is soft enough to mash, if not mince it before returning to the pan.
4. Add sour cream, chopped fresh chives, salt, and black pepper to the pot.
5. Mash the potatoes and garlic using a potato masher until smooth and creamy.
6. Taste and adjust seasoning if needed. If too thick, add water or milk a few teaspoons at a time (as this will be dependent on the starch content of the potatoes used).

Crispy Smashed Parmesan Potatoes

Ingredients:

- 750g baby potatoes
- 2 tablespoons olive oil
- Salt and black pepper to taste
- 100g finely grated parmesan cheese

Method:

1. Preheat the oven to 425°F (220°C).
2. Place the baby potatoes in a large pot of salted water and bring to a boil. Cook until the potatoes are fork-tender, about 15-20 minutes.
3. Drain the potatoes and let them cool slightly. Meanwhile, oil a baking tray and scatter the cheese over it.
4. Place the cooked potatoes on a plate and use the bottom of a glass or a potato masher to gently smash each potato until flattened but still intact. Now place onto the cheesy baking tray.
5. Drizzle olive oil over the smashed potatoes and season with salt and black pepper.
6. Bake in the preheated oven for 25-30 minutes, or until golden brown and crispy. Avoid the urge to shake or flip the potatoes as this will ruin the cheesy crust that's forming as they bake.

Potato Gratin

Ingredients:

- 750g large all rounder or waxy potatoes, peeled and thinly sliced OR
- 750g peeled and thinly sliced celeriac, fennel or swede (optional, great if you want to increase your plant intake)
- 150ml heavy cream
- 2 cloves garlic, minced
- 100g grated Gruyere cheese
- 2 tablespoons chopped fresh thyme
- Salt and black pepper to taste
- Butter for greasing the baking dish

Method:

1. Preheat the oven to 375°F (190°C). Grease a baking dish with butter.
2. Layer the thinly sliced potatoes in the prepared baking dish, overlapping slightly.
3. In a saucepan, heat the heavy cream and minced garlic over medium heat until it just begins to simmer.
4. Pour the hot cream mixture over the potatoes in the baking dish.
5. Sprinkle grated Gruyere cheese and chopped fresh thyme over the top.
6. Season with salt and black pepper.
7. Cover the baking dish with aluminium foil and bake in the preheated oven for 45 minutes.
8. Remove the foil and bake for an additional 15-20 minutes, or until the potatoes are tender and the top is golden brown and bubbly.
9. Let the Potato Gratin cool for a few minutes before serving. Reheats very well.

Easy but Impressive Hasselback Potatoes

Ingredients:

- 750g baby potatoes
- 4 tablespoons melted butter
- 4 cloves garlic, minced
- 2 tablespoons chopped fresh rosemary
- Salt and black pepper to taste

Method:

1. Preheat the oven to 425°F (220°C).
2. Slice each potato thinly but not all the way through, creating thin slices while keeping the potato intact. The best way to do this is to place a chopstick either side of the potato and then slice it down to that.
3. In a small bowl, mix together melted butter, minced garlic, chopped fresh rosemary, salt, and black pepper.
4. Place the sliced potatoes on a baking sheet lined with parchment paper.
5. Brush the butter mixture over the potatoes, making sure to get it between the slices.
6. Bake in the preheated oven for around 35 minutes, or until the potatoes are golden brown and crispy on the edges.

Fennel and Garlic Roasted Potato Wedges

Ingredients:

- 750g large white potatoes, scrubbed and cut into wedges OR you may choose to use sweet potatoes
- 3 tablespoons olive oil
- 4 cloves garlic, minced
- 1 teaspoon fennel seeds, well crushed
- Salt and black pepper to taste

Method:

1. Preheat the oven to 425°F (220°C).
2. In a large bowl, toss the potato wedges with olive oil, minced garlic, fennel, salt, and black pepper until evenly coated.
3. Spread the potato wedges in a single layer on a baking sheet.
4. Roast in the preheated oven for 30-35 minutes, flipping halfway through, until golden brown and crispy.

Sweet Potato Fries

Ingredients:

- 1kg sweet potatoes, peeled and cut into strips
- 3 tablespoons olive oil
- 1 teaspoon smoked paprika
- ½ teaspoon cumin
- Salt and black pepper to taste

Method:

1. Preheat the oven to 425°F (220°C).
2. In a large bowl, toss the sweet potato fries with olive oil, paprika, cumin, salt, and black pepper until evenly coated.
3. Spread the sweet potato fries in a single layer on a baking sheet lined with parchment paper.
4. Roast in the preheated oven for 25-30 minutes, flipping halfway through, until golden brown and crispy.

Lemon Herb Rice Pilaf

Ingredients:

- 200g long-grain white rice, well washed
- 400ml water or vegetable broth
- Zest of 1 lemon
- 2 tablespoons chopped fresh parsley
- 1 tablespoon chopped fresh dill
- 2 cardamom pods
- 2 tablespoons butter
- Salt and black pepper to taste

Method:

1. In a medium saucepan, toast the cardamom pods until fragrant then remove and set aside. Then melt the butter in this pan over medium heat.
2. Add the rice and cardamom to the saucepan and cook, stirring frequently for about 2 minutes.
3. Stir in the water or broth and lemon zest. Season with salt and black pepper.
4. Bring the mixture to a boil, then reduce the heat to low. Cover and simmer for 15-20 minutes, or until the rice is tender and the liquid is absorbed. Do not be tempted to remove the lid.
5. Remove the saucepan from heat and let it sit, covered, for 5 minutes.
6. Fluff the rice with a fork, then stir in the chopped fresh parsley and chopped fresh dill.

Coconut Jasmine Rice

Ingredients:

- 200g jasmine rice, well washed
- 400ml coconut milk
- 1 tablespoon sugar
- ½ teaspoon salt
- Optional garnish: toasted desiccated coconut (toast it in a dry pan until lightly brown then remove from heat) and chopped coriander/cilantro.

Method:

1. In a medium saucepan, combine the jasmine rice, coconut milk, water, sugar, and salt.
2. Bring the mixture to a boil over medium heat, then reduce the heat to low. Cover and simmer for 15-20 minutes, or until the rice is tender and the liquid is absorbed.
3. Remove the saucepan from heat and let it sit, covered, for 5 minutes.
4. Fluff the rice with a fork, then transfer it to a serving dish.
5. Garnish with toasted coconut and chopped fresh coriander/cilantro if desired.

Spanish Style Rice

Ingredients:

- 200g long-grain white rice, well washed
- 400ml water or broth
- 1 tablespoon olive oil
- ½ onion, finely chopped
- 1 red pepper, diced
- 2 cloves garlic, minced
- 1 teaspoon ground cumin
- 3 large tomatoes, chopped
- ½ teaspoon smoked paprika
- Salt and black pepper to taste
- 1/4 cup chopped fresh parsley

Method:

1. In a medium saucepan, heat the olive oil over medium heat. Add the chopped onion and diced red bell pepper. Cook until softened, about 5 minutes.
2. Stir in the minced garlic, ground cumin, and paprika. Cook for an additional 1-2 minutes, until fragrant.
3. Add the rice to the saucepan and cook, stirring frequently, for 2-3 minutes.
4. Pour in the water or broth and season with salt and black pepper. Add the tomatoes and bring the mixture to a boil.
5. Reduce the heat to low, cover, and simmer for 15-20 minutes, or until the rice is tender and the liquid is absorbed.
6. Remove the saucepan from heat and let it sit, covered, for 5 minutes.
7. Fluff the rice with a fork, then stir in the chopped fresh parsley.

Pineapple Fried Rice

Ingredients:

- 300g long-grain white rice, cooked and cooled (or some microwave rice packs are not UPF believe it or not)
- 2 tablespoons olive oil
- 2 eggs, beaten
- 150g diced pineapple
- 1 handful chopped spring onions
- 2 cloves garlic, minced
- 2 tablespoons soy sauce
- 1 tablespoon sesame oil
- 1 teaspoon Chinese 5 spice
- Salt and black pepper to taste
- Optional garnish: chopped fresh coriander/cilantro or thai basil, chopped cashews or peanuts

Method:

1. In a frying pan or wok, add a drizzle of oil and diced pineapple, garlic and chopped spring onions. Cook for 2-3 minutes, until heated through.
2. Add the cooked and cooled rice to the skillet or wok, breaking up any clumps with a spatula.
3. Pour soy sauce and sesame oil over the rice. Season with 5 spice, salt and black pepper to taste. Stir well to combine.
4. Make a well in the centre and add the eggs using a spatula or chopstick to scramble the egg mix. As it starts to set, toss everything together until evenly mixed and heated through.
5. Taste and adjust seasoning if needed.
6. Garnish with chopped fresh cilantro and chopped cashews or peanuts if desired.

Tomato Basil Rice

Ingredients:

- 200g long-grain white rice, well washed
- 400g tin chopped tomatoes
- 100ml water
- 1 large handful of chopped fresh basil
- 1 tablespoon olive oil
- 2 cloves garlic, minced
- 100g mascarpone (optional)
- Salt, sugar and black pepper to taste

Method:

1. In a medium saucepan, heat the olive oil over medium heat. Add the washed rice and minced garlic and cook for 1-2 minutes, until fragrant.
2. Add the tomatoes and water to the saucepan and bring the mixture to a boil. Add in a pinch of salt and sugar.
3. Reduce the heat to low, cover, and simmer for 15-20 minutes, or until the rice is tender and the liquid is absorbed.
4. Remove the saucepan from heat and let it sit, covered, for 5 minutes.
5. Fluff the rice with a fork, then stir in the chopped fresh basil and mascarpone if using.
6. Season with salt and black pepper to taste.

Double Baked Potatoes

Ingredients:

- 6 large white potatoes
- 2 tablespoons of butter
- 4 tablespoons of creme fraiche (optional)
- 100g grated cheese such as emmental or mild cheddar

Method:

1. Preheat oven to 200 degrees celsius. Once up to temperature add the potatoes and bake for 30 minutes.
2. Remove potatoes and cut in half. Scoop out the middle being careful not to damage the skin "shells" and mix with the butter, cheese and creme fraiche if using. You may add other toppings such as spring onions, cherry tomatoes etc if you like.
3. Return the filling to the potatoes and bake for a further 20 minutes. These reheat very well and are a good way to use up leftover veggies.

Main Proteins - Chicken

Lemon Garlic Roast Chicken

Ingredients:

- 1 whole chicken (about 1.6kg), giblets removed
- 2 lemons, halved
- 4 cloves garlic, minced
- 2 tablespoons olive oil
- 1 tablespoon chopped fresh rosemary
- Salt and black pepper to taste

Method:

1. Preheat the oven to 425°F (220°C).
2. Rinse the chicken inside and out, then pat dry with paper towels. Place the chicken in a roasting pan.
3. Rub the chicken all over with the halved lemons, squeezing the juice over the skin and inside the cavity.
4. In a small bowl, mix together minced garlic, olive oil, chopped fresh rosemary, salt, and black pepper.
5. Rub the garlic mixture all over the chicken, ensuring it's evenly coated.
6. Place the halved lemons inside the cavity of the chicken.
7. Roast in the preheated oven for about 1 hour and 15 minutes, or until the juices run clear and the skin is golden brown and crispy.
8. Remove the chicken from the oven and let it rest for 10-15 minutes before carving.

Chicken Piccata

Ingredients:

- 4 boneless, skinless chicken breasts
- Salt and black pepper to taste
- 100g cup all-purpose flour
- 2 tablespoons olive oil
- 4 tablespoons unsalted butter, divided
- 4 cloves garlic, minced
- 100ml chicken broth
- 1 fresh lemon, juiced
- 2 tablespoons capers, drained
- 2 tablespoons chopped fresh parsley
- Lemon slices for garnish

Method:

1. Season the chicken breasts with salt and black pepper on both sides.
2. Dredge the chicken breasts in flour, shaking off any excess.
3. In a large skillet, heat olive oil and 2 tablespoons of butter over medium-high heat.
4. Add the chicken breasts to the skillet and cook for 4-5 minutes per side, or until golden brown and cooked through. Remove the chicken from the skillet and set aside.
5. In the same skillet, add the minced garlic and cook for 1-2 minutes, until fragrant.
6. Pour in the chicken broth and lemon juice, scraping up any browned bits from the bottom of the skillet.
7. Bring the mixture to a simmer and cook for 2-3 minutes, until slightly reduced.
8. Stir in the remaining 2 tablespoons of butter and the drained capers. Cook for an additional 1-2 minutes, until the sauce thickens slightly.
9. Return the chicken breasts to the skillet and coat them

with the sauce.

10. Sprinkle chopped fresh parsley over the chicken.

Teriyaki Chicken Stir-Fry

Ingredients:

- 600g boneless, skinless chicken breasts, sliced into thin strips
- 2 tablespoons soy sauce
- 2 tablespoons honey
- 1 tablespoon rice vinegar or vinegar of choice
- 1 tablespoon sesame oil
- 2 cloves garlic, minced
- 1 teaspoon minced ginger
- 2 tablespoons olive oil
- 1 red pepper, thinly sliced
- 1 yellow pepper, thinly sliced
- Optional garnish: sesame seeds, chopped spring onions

Method:

1. In a small bowl, whisk together soy sauce, honey, rice vinegar, sesame oil, minced garlic, and minced ginger to make the teriyaki sauce.
2. In a large skillet or wok, heat olive oil over medium-high heat.
3. Add the peppers and sliced chicken breast to the skillet and cook until browned and cooked through, about 5-6 minutes. Remove the chicken from the skillet and set aside.
4. Pour the teriyaki sauce over the chicken.
5. Cook for an additional 1-2 minutes, until the sauce thickens slightly.
6. Remove from heat and garnish with sesame seeds and chopped spring onions if desired.

Smoky Paprika Butter Chicken

Ingredients:

- 600g boneless, skinless chicken breasts, sliced into strips
- 2 tablespoons butter
- 2 cloves garlic, minced
- 2 teaspoons smoked paprika powder
- 1 teaspoon ground cumin
- Salt and black pepper to taste
- Juice of 1 lime

Method:

1. In a large skillet or cast-iron pan, heat butter, paprika and cumin over medium-high heat.
2. Add the sliced chicken breast and garlic to the skillet and cook until chicken is browned and cooked through, about 5-6 minutes.
3. Season with salt and pepper and fresh lime juice.

Chicken and Vegetable Skewers

Ingredients:

- 600g boneless, skinless chicken breasts, cut into bite-sized pieces and marinated in natural yoghurt for at least 1 hour before cooking
- 1 red pepper, cut into chunks
- 1 yellow pepper, cut into chunks
- 1 red onion, cut into chunks
- 1 courgette, sliced into rounds
- 2 tablespoons olive oil
- 2 cloves garlic, minced
- 1 teaspoon dried oregano
- 1 teaspoon dried thyme
- 1 teaspoon smoked paprika
- Salt and black pepper to taste
- Wooden or metal skewers

Method:

1. If using wooden skewers, soak them in water for at least 30 minutes to prevent burning.
2. In a large bowl, combine marinated chicken breast pieces, bell pepper chunks, onion chunks, and courgette slices.
3. In a small bowl, whisk together olive oil, minced garlic, dried oregano, dried thyme, smoked paprika, salt, and black pepper to make the sauce.
4. Pour the sauce over the chicken and vegetables, coating everything evenly.
5. Preheat the grill or grill pan over medium-high heat.
6. Thread the marinated chicken and vegetables onto skewers, alternating the pieces.
7. Grill the skewers for 8-10 minutes, turning occasionally, until the chicken is cooked through and the vegetables are tender.

8. Remove from the grill and serve.

Chicken and Spinach Stuffed Portobello Mushrooms

Ingredients:

- 4 large Portobello mushrooms, stems removed
- 200g minced chicken
- 50g fresh baby spinach leaves
- 3 tablespoons tomato puree
- 1 ball of torn mozzarella cheese (avoid pre grated harder mozzarella as they are often coated in an anti caking agent)
- 2 tablespoons grated parmesan cheese
- 2 cloves garlic, minced
- 2 tablespoons olive oil
- Salt and black pepper to taste
- Chopped fresh basil for garnish

Method:

1. Preheat the oven to 375°F (190°C). Grease a baking dish with olive oil.
2. Place the Portobello mushrooms in the prepared baking dish, gill side up.
3. In a large skillet, heat olive oil over medium heat. Add chicken, spinach and minced garlic and cook for until chicken is cooked through, around 6-8 minutes.
4. Remove from heat and stir in marinara sauce, shredded mozzarella cheese, and grated Parmesan cheese. Season with salt and black pepper to taste.
5. Spoon the chicken and spinach mixture into the Portobello mushrooms, dividing it evenly among them.
6. Bake in the preheated oven for 10-15, or until the mushrooms are tender and the cheese is melted and bubbly.
7. Remove from the oven and garnish with chopped fresh basil.

Chicken and Mushroom Marsala

Ingredients:

- 4 boneless, skinless chicken breasts
- Salt and black pepper to taste
- 100g cup all-purpose flour
- 2 tablespoons olive oil
- 2 tablespoons unsalted butter
- 100g chestnut or wild mushrooms, sliced
- 2 cloves garlic, minced
- 1 cup Marsala wine
- 1 cup fresh chicken stock or water or single cream
- 2 tablespoons chopped fresh parsley

Method:

1. Season the chicken breasts with salt and black pepper on both sides.
2. Dredge the chicken breasts in flour, shaking off any excess.
3. In a large skillet, heat olive oil and butter over medium-high heat.
4. Add the chicken breasts to the skillet and cook for 4-5 minutes per side, or until golden brown and cooked through. Remove the chicken from the skillet and set aside.
5. In the same skillet, add sliced mushrooms and minced garlic. Cook for 5-6 minutes, or until the mushrooms are golden brown and tender.
6. Pour Marsala wine into the skillet, scraping up any browned bits from the bottom of the skillet.
7. Cook for 2-3 minutes, allowing the wine to reduce slightly.
8. Stir in chicken broth and chopped fresh parsley. Bring the mixture to a simmer.

9. Return the cooked chicken breasts to the skillet and coat them with the Marsala sauce.
10. Cook for an additional 2-3 minutes, until everything is cooked through.

Quick Crispy Chicken

Ingredients:

- 4 boneless, skinless chicken breasts made thinner by slicing lengthways
- Salt and black pepper to taste
- 100g all-purpose plain flour
- 2 large eggs, beaten
- 1 cup breadcrumbs (we buy Crosta & Mollica breadsticks and bash them up!)
- 50g grated Parmesan cheese
- 2 tablespoons olive oil
- Chopped fresh basil for garnish

Method:

1. Preheat the oven to 400°F (200°C). Grease a baking dish with olive oil.
2. Season the chicken breasts with salt and black pepper on both sides.
3. Dredge the chicken breasts in flour, shaking off any excess.
4. Dip the chicken breasts into the beaten eggs, then coat them with a mixture of breadcrumbs and grated Parmesan cheese, pressing gently to adhere.
5. In a large skillet, heat olive oil over medium-high heat.
6. Add the coated chicken breasts to the skillet and cook for 3-4 minutes per side, or until golden brown and crispy. Remove from the skillet and transfer to the prepared baking dish.
7. Cover with foil and bake in the preheated oven for 20-25 minutes, or until the chicken is cooked through.
8. Remove from the oven and garnish with chopped fresh basil.

Honey and Garlic Sesame Chicken Thighs

Ingredients:

- 2kg bone-in, skin-on chicken thighs
- Salt and black pepper to taste
- 4 tablespoons olive oil
- 4 cloves garlic, minced
- 6 tablespoons honey
- 4 tablespoons soy sauce
- 2 tablespoon rice vinegar or vinegar of your choice
- 2 teaspoons sesame oil
- 3 teaspoons sesame seeds
- 1 tablespoon chopped spring onions for garnish

Method:

1. Preheat the oven to 400°F (200°C).
2. Season the chicken thighs with salt and black pepper on both sides.
3. In a large ovenproof skillet, heat olive oil over medium-high heat.
4. Add the chicken thighs to the skillet, skin side down, and cook for 5-6 minutes until browned and crispy. Flip and cook for another 2-3 minutes.
5. In a small bowl, mix minced garlic, honey, soy sauce, rice vinegar, and sesame oil.
6. Pour the honey garlic sauce over the chicken thighs, coating them evenly. Sprinkle the sesame seeds over the top.
7. Transfer to the preheated oven and bake for 20-25 minutes, or until the chicken thighs are cooked through and the sauce is caramelised.
8. Garnish with chopped spring onions before serving.

Balsamic Glazed Chicken Thighs

Ingredients:

- 2kg bone-in, skin-on chicken thighs
- Salt and black pepper to taste
- 2 tablespoons olive oil
- 2 tablespoons balsamic vinegar
- 2 tablespoons honey
- 2 cloves garlic, minced
- 1 teaspoon dried thyme
- Chopped fresh parsley for garnish

Method:

1. Preheat the oven to 400°F (200°C).
2. Season the chicken thighs with salt and black pepper on both sides.
3. In a large ovenproof pan (if you have one, otherwise just use a regular pan and transfer to a baking tray after), heat olive oil over medium-high heat.
4. Add the chicken thighs to the skillet, skin side down, and cook for 5-6 minutes until browned and crispy. Flip and cook for another 2-3 minutes.
5. In a small bowl, mix balsamic vinegar, honey, minced garlic, and dried thyme.
6. Pour the balsamic glaze over the chicken thighs, coating them evenly.
7. Transfer the skillet to the preheated oven and bake for 20-25 minutes, or until the chicken thighs are cooked through and the glaze is caramelised.
8. Garnish with chopped fresh parsley before serving.

Coconut Curry Chicken Thighs

Ingredients:

- 2kg bone-in, skin-on chicken thighs
- Salt and black pepper to taste
- 2 tablespoons olive oil
- 1 onion, chopped
- 2 cloves garlic, minced
- 1 tablespoon minced ginger
- 2 tablespoons mild curry powder
- 1 x 400g tin coconut milk
- 2 cups chopped vegetables (such as peppers, carrots, and potatoes)
- Chopped fresh coriander/cilantro for garnish

Method:

1. Season the chicken thighs with salt and black pepper on both sides.
2. In a large pan, heat olive oil over medium-high heat before adding the chicken thighs, skin side down. Cook for 5-6 minutes until browned and crispy. Flip and cook for another 2-3 minutes. Remove from the pan and set aside.
3. In the same skillet, add chopped onion, minced garlic, and minced ginger. Cook for 2-3 minutes until softened and fragrant.
4. Sprinkle in the curry powder and cook for another minute.
5. Pour in coconut milk, stirring to combine.
6. Add chopped vegetables to the skillet and bring the mixture to a simmer.
7. Return the chicken thighs to the skillet, nestling them into the sauce and vegetables.
8. Cover and let it simmer for 20-25 minutes, or until the chicken thighs are cooked through and the vegetables are tender.

9. Garnish with chopped fresh cilantro before serving.

Maple Apple Chicken Thighs

Ingredients:

- 2kg bone-in, skin-on chicken thighs
- Salt and black pepper to taste
- 2 tablespoons olive oil
- 2 tablespoons pure maple syrup
- 2 cloves garlic, minced
- 1 tablespoon apple cider vinegar
- 2 large cooking apples, thinly sliced

Method:

1. Season the chicken thighs with salt and black pepper on both sides.
2. In a large pan, heat olive oil over medium-high heat and add the chicken thighs skin side down. Cook for 5-6 minutes until browned and crispy. Flip and cook for another 2-3 minutes.
3. Remove excess fat from the skillet, leaving about 1 tablespoon.
4. In a small bowl, mix sliced apples, maple syrup, minced garlic, and apple cider vinegar.
5. Place chicken thighs onto a greased roasting tray and pour the mixture over the chicken thighs, coating them evenly and allowing the apples to fall onto the tray.
6. Roast for 20-25 minutes, or until the chicken thighs are cooked through.

Lebanese 7 Spice Marinated Chicken Kebabs

Ingredients:

For the marinade:

- 1kg boneless, skinless chicken breasts or thighs (we prefer thigh meat for this)
- 150g plain Greek yoghurt
- 2 tablespoons olive oil
- 2 cloves garlic, minced
- 1 tablespoon Lebanese 7 spice blend (a mix of allspice, black pepper, cinnamon, cloves, nutmeg, fenugreek, and ginger)
- Juice of 1 lemon
- Salt and pepper to taste

For assembling the kebabs:

- Bamboo skewers, 2 or 3, soaked in water for at least 30 minutes
- Red onion, cut in half for skewering with the chicken

Instructions:

1. Prepare the Marinade:

In a large mixing bowl, combine the Greek yoghurt, olive oil, minced garlic, Lebanese 7 spice blend, lemon juice, salt, and pepper. Mix the marinade ingredients until well combined.

2. Marinate the Chicken:

Add the chicken chunks to the marinade and toss until they are evenly coated. Cover the bowl with plastic wrap or transfer the mixture to a resealable plastic bag. Place the marinated chicken in the refrigerator and let it marinate for at least 2 hours, or preferably overnight, to allow the flavours to meld together.

3. Assemble the Kebabs and Preheat Oven:

Once the chicken has finished marinating, remove it from the refrigerator. Preheat your oven to 200 degrees celsius and ensure there is enough room for the tray to sit near the bottom with the kebab standing on top. Stick the skewers into the onion half to create a support that should stand up (although it can also cook very nicely on its side). The onion is there to stop the chicken falling off the skewers. Thread the marinated chicken onto the soaked bamboo skewers and push down as you go. You should end up with what looks like a mini kebab house kebab that stands up on a tray in the oven.

4. Cook the Kebabs:

Roast in the oven for 35-45 minutes until the chicken is cooked through. Check by ensuring the juices run clear. Once cooked, serve with salad and flatbread.

Mains - Pork

Honey Chilli Glazed Pork Chops

Ingredients:

- 1kg bone-in pork chops
- Salt and black pepper to taste
- 2 tablespoons olive oil
- 4 teaspoons honey
- 2 teaspoons fresh chopped red chilli
- 1 tablespoon apple cider vinegar or vinegar of choice
- 2 cloves garlic, minced
- Chopped fresh parsley for garnish

Method:

1. Season the pork chops with salt and black pepper on both sides.
2. In a small bowl, mix together honey, chilli, vinegar and minced garlic to make the glaze.
3. In a large skillet, heat olive oil over medium-high heat.
4. Add the pork chops to the skillet and cook for 3 minutes per side.
5. Brush the honey mustard glaze over the pork chops and cook for 2 more minutes or until pork is cooked through.
6. Remove the pork chops from the skillet and let them rest for a few minutes before serving. Garnish with chopped fresh parsley.

Garlic Herb Roasted Pork Tenderloin

Ingredients:

- 500g pork tenderloin
- Salt and black pepper to taste
- 2 tablespoons olive oil
- 4 cloves garlic, minced
- 1 tablespoon chopped fresh rosemary
- 1 tablespoon chopped fresh thyme
- 1 tablespoon chopped fresh parsley
- Lemon wedges for serving

Method:

1. Preheat the oven to 400°F (200°C).
2. Season the pork tenderloin with salt and black pepper on all sides.
3. In a small bowl, mix minced garlic, chopped fresh rosemary, chopped fresh thyme, and chopped fresh parsley.
4. Rub the garlic herb mixture evenly over the pork tenderloin.
5. In an ovenproof pan/skillet, heat olive oil over medium-high heat.
6. Add the pork tenderloin to the skillet and sear on all sides until browned, about 2-3 minutes per side.
7. Transfer the skillet to the preheated oven and roast for 15-20 minutes, or until the internal temperature of the pork reaches 145°F (63°C).
8. Remove from the oven and rest for a few minutes before slicing. Serve with lemon wedges.

Maple Glazed Pork Belly

Ingredients:

- 500g pork belly, skin removed and cut into slices
- Salt and black pepper to taste
- 2 tablespoons olive oil
- 3 tablespoons maple syrup (or honey)
- 2 tablespoons soy sauce
- 2 cloves garlic, minced
- 1 thumb sized piece of ginger, grated
- Sesame seeds for garnish
- Sliced spring onions for garnish

Method:

1. Season the pork belly slices with salt and black pepper on both sides.
2. In a small bowl, mix together maple syrup, soy sauce, minced garlic, and grated fresh ginger to make the glaze.
3. In a large frying pan/skillet, heat olive oil over medium-high heat.
4. Add the pork belly slices to the skillet and cook for 3-4 minutes per side, or until browned and caramelised.
5. Pour the maple glaze over the pork belly slices, coating them evenly.
6. Cook for an additional 2-3 minutes, allowing the glaze to thicken slightly.
7. Remove from the skillet and transfer to a serving plate. Garnish with sesame seeds and spring onion.

Apple Cider Pork Chops

Ingredients:

- 1kg bone-in pork chops
- Salt and black pepper to taste
- 2 tablespoons olive oil
- 250ml medium apple cider
- 2 tablespoons double cream (optional)
- 2 tablespoons honey
- 2 cloves garlic, minced
- 1 teaspoon dried thyme
- Apple slices, ideally a tart variety

Method:

1. Season the pork chops with salt and black pepper on both sides.
2. In a small bowl, mix together apple cider, cream (if using), honey, minced garlic, and dried thyme.
3. In a large frying pan/skillet, heat olive oil over medium-high heat.
4. Add the pork chops to the skillet and cook for 3-4 minutes per side, or until browned.
5. Pour the apple cider mixture and apple slices over the pork chops, coating them evenly.
6. Reduce the heat to medium-low and simmer for 10-12 minutes, or until the pork chops are cooked through and the sauce has thickened.

Rosemary Balsamic Pork Tenderloin

Ingredients:

- 500g pork tenderloin
- Salt and black pepper to taste
- 2 tablespoons olive oil
- 3 tablespoons balsamic vinegar
- 2 tablespoons honey
- 2 cloves garlic, minced
- 1 tablespoon chopped fresh rosemary
- Chopped fresh parsley for garnish

Method:

1. Preheat the oven to 400°F (200°C).
2. Season the pork tenderloin with salt and black pepper on all sides.
3. In a small bowl, mix together balsamic vinegar, honey, minced garlic, and chopped fresh rosemary.
4. In an ovenproof skillet, heat olive oil over medium-high heat.
5. Add the pork tenderloin to the skillet and sear on all sides until browned, about 2-3 minutes per side.
6. Pour the balsamic mixture over the pork tenderloin, coating it evenly.
7. Transfer the skillet to the preheated oven and roast for 15-20 minutes, or until the internal temperature of the pork reaches 145°F (63°C).
8. Remove from the oven and let the pork tenderloin rest for a few minutes before slicing.
9. Garnish with chopped fresh parsley before serving.

Pineapple Teriyaki Pork Skewers

Ingredients:

- 500g pork tenderloin, cut into cubes
- Salt and black pepper to taste
- 500g pineapple, cut into chunks
- 1 red pepper, cut into chunks
- 1 onion, cut into chunks
- Wooden skewers, soaked in water for 30 minutes or metal skewers
- Sesame seeds for garnish

For the Teriyaki Style Marinade:

- 3 tablespoons cup soy sauce
- 2 tablespoons honey
- 2 tablespoons rice vinegar or vinegar of choice
- 1 teaspoon Chinese 5 spice
- 1 tablespoon sesame oil
- 2 cloves garlic, minced
- 1 teaspoon grated fresh ginger

Method:

1. Season the pork tenderloin cubes with salt and black pepper.
2. In a bowl, combine all the ingredients for the teriyaki marinade.
3. Add the pork cubes to the marinade and let them marinate in the refrigerator for at least 30 minutes.
4. Preheat the grill to medium-high heat.
5. Thread the marinated pork cubes onto the soaked wooden skewers, alternating with pineapple chunks, bell pepper, and onion.
6. Grill the skewers for 10-12 minutes, turning occasionally, until the pork is cooked through and the vegetables are

charred.

7. Remove from the grill and let them rest for a few minutes.
8. Garnish with sesame seeds before serving.

Mains - Lamb

Quick Greek-Style Lamb

Ingredients:

For the Lamb:

- 500g lamb leg steaks, thinly sliced
- Salt and black pepper to taste
- 2 tablespoons olive oil

- 2 cloves garlic, minced
- 1 tablespoon dried oregano
- Juice of 1 lemon

For the Tzatziki Sauce:

- 100ml Greek yoghurt
- 1 cucumber, grated and squeezed to remove excess moisture
- 2 cloves garlic, minced
- 1 tablespoon chopped fresh dill
- Salt and black pepper to taste

Method:

1. Season the thinly sliced lamb with salt, black pepper, minced garlic, dried oregano, and lemon juice. Let it marinate for at least 30 minutes.
2. In a bowl, combine Greek yoghurt, grated cucumber, minced garlic, chopped fresh dill, salt, and black pepper to make the tzatziki sauce. Refrigerate until ready to use.
3. Heat olive oil in a skillet over medium-high heat. Add the marinated lamb slices and cook for 3-4 minutes per side until browned and cooked through.
4. Garnish with chopped fresh parsley and the tzatziki sauce before serving.

Moroccan Spiced Lamb

Ingredients:

- 500g lamb stew meat, cubed
- Salt and black pepper to taste
- 2 tablespoons olive oil
- 1 onion, chopped
- 2 cloves garlic, minced
- 1 tablespoon ground cumin
- 1 tablespoon ground coriander
- 1 teaspoon ground cinnamon
- 1/2 teaspoon ground ginger
- 1/4 teaspoon ground cloves
- 1/4 teaspoon ground nutmeg
- 1 x 400g tin diced tomatoes
- 150ml water with ½ tsp salt added
- 1 cup dried apricots, chopped
- 1/4 cup sliced almonds
- Chopped fresh coriander/cilantro or parsley for garnish

Method:

1. Season the lamb stew meat with salt and black pepper.
2. In a large pan, heat olive oil over medium heat. Add the chopped onion and minced garlic, and cook until softened and fragrant.
3. Add the seasoned lamb cubes to the tagine and brown on all sides.
4. Sprinkle ground cumin, ground coriander, ground cinnamon, ground ginger, ground cloves, and ground nutmeg over the lamb, stirring to coat evenly.
5. Pour in diced tomatoes and salted water. Stir well to combine.
6. Bring the mixture to a simmer, then cover and cook over low heat for 1.5 to 2 hours, or until the lamb is tender.

7. Stir in chopped dried apricots and sliced almonds during the last 15 minutes of cooking.
8. Garnish with chopped fresh coriander/cilantro or parsley before serving.

Grilled Lamb Kofta

Ingredients:

- 500g minced lamb
- 1 onion, finely chopped
- 2 cloves garlic, minced
- 1 tablespoon chopped fresh parsley
- 1 tablespoon chopped fresh mint
- 1 teaspoon ground cumin
- 1 teaspoon ground coriander
- 1/2 teaspoon ground cinnamon
- Salt and black pepper to taste
- Wooden skewers, soaked in water for 30 minutes

- Lemon wedges for serving

Method:

1. In a bowl, combine ground lamb, grated onion, minced garlic, chopped fresh parsley, chopped fresh mint, ground cumin, ground coriander, ground cinnamon, salt, and black pepper. Mix well to combine.
2. Divide the lamb mixture into equal portions and form each portion around a wooden skewer to make kofta shapes.
3. Preheat the grill to medium-high heat.
4. Grill the lamb koftas for 5-6 minutes per side, or until cooked through and browned on the outside.
5. Serve the grilled lamb koftas with lemon wedges for squeezing over them before serving.

Lamb and Spinach Stuffed Peppers

Ingredients:

- 4 red or green peppers
- 500g minced lamb
- Salt and black pepper to taste
- 2 tablespoons olive oil
- 1 onion, chopped
- 2 cloves garlic, minced
- 100g fresh spinach, chopped
- 200g cooked rice (or UPF free microwave rice)
- 100g crumbled feta cheese
- Chopped fresh parsley for garnish

Method:

1. Preheat the oven to 375°F (190°C).
2. Cut the tops off the bell peppers and remove the seeds and membranes from the insides.
3. Season the inside of the bell peppers with salt and black pepper.
4. In a frying pan, heat olive oil over medium heat. Add chopped onion and cook until softened.
5. Add minced garlic and cook for another minute.
6. Add ground lamb to the pan and cook until browned.
7. Stir in chopped fresh spinach and cook until wilted.
8. Remove the skillet from the heat and stir in cooked rice and crumbled feta cheese.
9. Spoon the lamb and spinach mixture into the bell peppers.
10. Place the stuffed bell peppers in a baking dish and cover with foil.
11. Bake in the preheated oven for 25-30 minutes, or until the bell peppers are tender.
12. Garnish with chopped fresh parsley before serving.

Garlic and Rosemary Roast Leg of Lamb

Ingredients:

- 1 leg of lamb, bone-in approx 1.5kg
- Salt and black pepper to taste
- 6 cloves garlic, thinly sliced
- 4 tablespoons chopped fresh rosemary
- 2 tablespoons olive oil
- 1 cup dry red wine
- 1 cup beef or vegetable broth

Method:

1. Preheat the oven to 375°F (190°C).
2. Season the leg of lamb with salt and black pepper.
3. Make small incisions all over the leg of lamb and insert the thinly sliced garlic and chopped fresh rosemary into the incisions.
4. Rub the leg of lamb with olive oil.
5. Place the leg of lamb in a roasting pan and pour the dry red wine and broth into the pan.
6. Roast in the preheated oven for about 1.5 to 2 hours, or until the internal temperature reaches your desired level of doneness (145°F for medium-rare, 160°F for medium, or 170°F for well-done). Baste the lamb occasionally with the pan juices.
7. Remove from the oven and let it rest for about 15 minutes before slicing.
8. Serve the sliced leg of lamb with the pan juices.

Mains - Fish & Seafood

Lemon Herb Grilled Salmon

Ingredients:

- 4 wild salmon fillets
- Salt and black pepper to taste
- 2 tablespoons olive oil
- Zest and juice of 1 lemon
- 2 cloves garlic, minced
- 2 tablespoons chopped fresh parsley
- 1 tablespoon chopped fresh dill

Method:

1. In a small bowl, whisk together olive oil, lemon zest, lemon juice, minced garlic, chopped fresh parsley, and chopped fresh dill to make a marinade.
2. Place the salmon fillets in a shallow dish and pour the marinade over them, coating evenly. Let them marinate for about 15-30 minutes.Preheat a frying pan to medium-high heat.
3. Remove the salmon fillets from the marinade and place them on the preheated grill.
4. Pan fry for 4-5 minutes on the skin side until the skin is no longer stuck. Turn the salmon and cook for another 3-4 minutes on the other side until cooked through.

Honey Soy Glazed Salmon

Ingredients:

- 4 wild salmon fillets
- Salt and black pepper to taste
- 3 tablespoons soy sauce
- 2 tablespoons honey
- 2 cloves garlic, minced
- 1 tablespoon grated ginger
- 1 tablespoon olive oil
- Sliced spring onions for garnish

Method:

1. Preheat the oven to 400°F (200°C).
2. Season the salmon fillets with salt and black pepper.
3. In a small bowl, whisk together soy sauce, honey, minced garlic, grated ginger, and olive oil to make a glaze.
4. Place the salmon fillets on a baking sheet lined with parchment paper.
5. Brush the glaze over the salmon fillets, coating them evenly.
6. Bake in the preheated oven for 12-15 minutes, or until the salmon is cooked through and flakes easily with a fork.
7. Garnish with sliced green onions before serving.

Spice Crusted Salmon

Ingredients:

- 4 salmon fillets
- Salt and black pepper to taste
- 2 tablespoons olive oil

For the Spice Crust:

- 1 tablespoon ground cumin
- 1 tablespoon paprika
- 1 teaspoon ground coriander
- 1 teaspoon ground turmeric
- 1 teaspoon ground cinnamon
- 1/2 teaspoon cayenne pepper (adjust to taste)
- Lemon wedges to serve

Method:

1. Preheat the oven to 400°F (200°C). Line a baking sheet with parchment paper.
2. In a small bowl, mix together all the spices to create the spice crust mixture.
3. Pat the salmon fillets dry with paper towels and season them generously with salt and black pepper.
4. Rub each salmon fillet with olive oil, ensuring they are coated evenly.
5. Sprinkle the spice crust mixture over the top of each salmon fillet, pressing gently to adhere the spices.
6. Place the seasoned salmon fillets on the prepared baking sheet.
7. Bake in the preheated oven for 12-15 minutes, or until the salmon is cooked through and flakes easily with a fork.
8. Once done, remove the salmon from the oven and let it rest for a few minutes before serving.
9. Serve with lemon wedges.

Tikka Salmon

Ingredients:

- 4 wild salmon fillets
- Salt to taste
- 1 tablespoon olive oil

For the Tikka Marinade:

- 150ml cup plain yoghurt
- 2 tablespoons tomato paste
- 1 tablespoon lemon juice
- 1 tablespoon minced ginger
- 1 tablespoon minced garlic
- 1 teaspoon ground coriander
- 1 teaspoon ground cumin
- 1/2 teaspoon ground turmeric
- 1/2 teaspoon paprika
- 1/4 teaspoon cayenne pepper (adjust to taste)
- Salt to taste
- Fresh coriander/cilantro, chopped (for garnish)

Method:

1. Preheat the oven to 400°F (200°C). Line a baking sheet with parchment paper.
2. Pat the salmon fillets dry with paper towels and season them with salt.
3. In a mixing bowl, combine all the ingredients for the tikka marinade: yoghurt, tomato paste, lemon juice, minced ginger, minced garlic, ground coriander, ground cumin, ground turmeric, paprika, cayenne pepper, and salt. Mix well to combine.
4. Place the salmon fillets in a shallow dish or a resealable plastic bag. Pour the tikka marinade over the salmon, ensuring they are well coated. Marinate in the refrigerator

for at least 30 minutes, or up to 2 hours for maximum flavour.

5. Remove the salmon fillets from the marinade and place them on the prepared baking sheet.
6. Drizzle olive oil over the salmon fillets.
7. Bake in the preheated oven for 12-15 minutes, or until the salmon is cooked through and flakes easily with a fork.
8. Once done, remove the salmon from the oven and let it rest for a few minutes before garnishing and serving.

Citrus Miso Salmon

Ingredients:

- 4 salmon fillets
- Salt and black pepper to taste
- 2 tablespoons white miso paste (we like Yutaka brand)
- 2 tablespoons honey
- 2 tablespoons orange juice
- 1 tablespoon lemon juice
- 1 tablespoon lime juice
- 1 tablespoon soy sauce
- 2 cloves garlic, minced
- 1 teaspoon grated ginger
- 1 tablespoon sesame oil
- Sesame seeds, for garnish
- Sliced spring onions, for garnish

Method:

1. Preheat the oven to 400°F (200°C). Line a baking sheet with parchment paper.
2. Season the salmon fillets with salt and black pepper, then place them on the prepared baking sheet.
3. In a small bowl, whisk together the white miso paste, honey, orange juice, lemon juice, lime juice, soy sauce, minced garlic, grated ginger, and sesame oil to make the marinade.
4. Pour the marinade over the salmon fillets, ensuring they are well coated. Let them marinate for about 15-30 minutes.
5. Once marinated, transfer the baking sheet to the preheated oven.
6. Bake the salmon for 12-15 minutes, or until it is cooked through and flakes easily with a fork.
7. Remove the salmon from the oven and let it rest for a few

minutes.

8. Garnish the Citrus Miso Salmon with sesame seeds and sliced spring onions before serving.

Citrus Sea Bass

Ingredients:

- 4 sea bass fillets
- Salt and black pepper to taste
- 2 tablespoons olive oil
- Zest and juice of 1 lemon
- Zest and juice of 1 lime
- Zest and juice of 1 orange
- 2 cloves garlic, minced
- 1 tablespoon chopped fresh parsley
- 1 tablespoon chopped fresh coriander/cilantro
- 1 tablespoon chopped fresh chives
- Lemon slices, for garnish
- Lime slices, for garnish
- Orange slices, for garnish

Method:

1. Preheat the oven to 375°F (190°C). Line a baking dish with parchment paper.
2. Season the sea bass fillets with salt and black pepper on both sides.
3. In a small bowl, whisk together the olive oil, lemon zest and juice, lime zest and juice, orange zest and juice, minced garlic, chopped fresh parsley, chopped fresh cilantro, and chopped fresh chives to make the marinade.
4. Place the sea bass fillets in the prepared baking dish.
5. Pour the marinade over the sea bass fillets, ensuring they are well coated. Let them marinate for about 15-30 minutes.
6. Once marinated, place a few slices of lemon, lime, and orange on top of each sea bass fillet.
7. Bake in the preheated oven for 15-20 minutes, or until the sea bass is cooked through and flakes easily with a fork.

8. Remove from the oven and garnish with additional chopped fresh herbs if desired.

Cod Milanese with Chili & Orange Dressing

Ingredients:

For the Cod Milanese:

- 4 cod fillets
- Salt and black pepper to taste
- 100g plain all-purpose flour
- 2 eggs, beaten
- 1 cup breadcrumbs (we use Crosta & Mollica breadsticks that have had a good bashing)
- 2 tablespoons grated Parmesan cheese
- 2 tablespoons olive oil

For the Chili & Orange Dressing:

- Zest and juice of 1 orange
- 1 red chilli, finely chopped
- 2 tablespoons olive oil
- 1 tablespoon honey
- Salt and black pepper to taste
- Fresh parsley, chopped (for garnish)

Method:

1. Preheat the oven to 400°F (200°C). Line a baking sheet with parchment paper.
2. Season the cod fillets with salt and black pepper on both sides.
3. Set up three shallow bowls: one with flour, one with beaten eggs, and one with breadcrumbs mixed with grated Parmesan cheese.
4. Dredge each cod fillet in the flour, shaking off any excess. Then dip them into the beaten eggs, followed by the breadcrumb mixture, pressing gently to adhere.
5. Place the breaded cod fillets on the prepared baking sheet.

6. Drizzle olive oil over the top of each cod fillet.
7. Bake in the preheated oven for 12-15 minutes, or until the cod is cooked through and the breadcrumbs are golden brown and crispy.
8. While the cod is baking, prepare the chilli & orange dressing. In a small bowl, whisk together the orange zest, orange juice, finely chopped red chilli, olive oil, honey, salt, and black pepper.
9. Once the cod is done baking, remove it from the oven and transfer it to serving plates.
10. Drizzle the chilli & orange dressing over the cod fillets.
11. Garnish with chopped fresh parsley.

Baked Paprika Cod

Ingredients:

- 4 cod fillets
- Salt and black pepper to taste
- 2 tablespoons olive oil
- 2 teaspoons paprika
- 1 teaspoon garlic powder
- 1 teaspoon onion powder
- 1/2 teaspoon dried thyme
- 1/2 teaspoon dried oregano
- 1/2 teaspoon smoked paprika
- 1/4 teaspoon cayenne pepper (optional for extra heat)
- Lemon wedges, for serving

Method:

1. Preheat the oven to 400°F (200°C). Line a baking sheet with parchment paper.
2. Pat the cod fillets dry with paper towels and place them on the prepared baking sheet.
3. In a small bowl, mix together the olive oil, paprika, garlic powder, onion powder, dried thyme, dried oregano, smoked paprika, and cayenne pepper (if using) to make a spice rub.
4. Brush both sides of the cod fillets with the spice rub, ensuring they are evenly coated.
5. Bake in the preheated oven for 12-15 minutes, or until the cod is cooked through and flakes easily with a fork.
6. Once done, remove the cod from the oven and let it rest for a few minutes.
7. Serve the Baked Paprika Cod hot with lemon wedges for squeezing over the top.

Turmeric Cod

Ingredients:

- 4 cod fillets
- Salt and black pepper to taste
- 2 tablespoons olive oil
- 2 teaspoons ground turmeric
- 1 teaspoon ground cumin
- 1 teaspoon ground coriander
- 1/2 teaspoon paprika
- 1/2 teaspoon garlic powder
- 1/2 teaspoon onion powder
- Lemon wedges, for serving
- Fresh coriander/cilantro, chopped, for garnish

Method:

1. Preheat the oven to 400°F (200°C). Line a baking sheet with parchment paper.
2. Pat the cod fillets dry with paper towels and place them on the prepared baking sheet.
3. In a small bowl, mix together the olive oil, ground turmeric, ground cumin, ground coriander, paprika, garlic powder, and onion powder to make a spice rub.
4. Brush both sides of the cod fillets with the spice rub, ensuring they are evenly coated.
5. Bake in the preheated oven for 12-15 minutes, or until the cod is cooked through and flakes easily with a fork.
6. Once done, remove the cod from the oven and let it rest for a few minutes. Serve with lemon wedges.

Marinated Smoked Mackerel

Ingredients:

- 4 smoked mackerel fillets
- 1/4 cup olive oil
- 1 lemon, juice and zest (unwaxed)
- 1 orange, juice and zest (unwaxed)
- 2 cloves garlic, minced
- 1 teaspoon honey
- 1 tablespoon chopped fresh dill
- Salt and black pepper to taste
- Lemon wedges, for serving
- Fresh dill sprigs, for garnish

Method:

1. In a small bowl, whisk together the olive oil, lemon and orange juice, minced garlic, honey, and dill to make the marinade.
2. Season the smoked mackerel fillets with salt and black pepper.
3. Place the mackerel fillets in a shallow dish or a resealable plastic bag.
4. Pour the marinade over the mackerel fillets, ensuring they are well coated. Cover or seal the dish/bag and refrigerate for at least 30 minutes, or up to 2 hours to allow the flavours to develop.
5. After marinating, remove the mackerel fillets from the refrigerator and let them come to room temperature for about 10 minutes.
6. Heat a grill pan or skillet over medium-high heat. Remove the mackerel fillets from the marinade and shake off any excess.
7. Place the mackerel fillets in the heated pan, skin side down, and cook for 1-2 minutes on each side until heated through

and lightly charred.

8. Once done, remove the mackerel fillets from the pan and transfer them to a serving plate.
9. Serve garnished with lemon wedges and fresh dill sprigs.

Spicy Tuna Larb

Ingredients:

- 2 small tins of tuna in water, drained
- 2 tablespoons fish sauce (optional)
- 2 tablespoons lime juice
- 1 tablespoon soy sauce
- 1 tablespoon honey
- 1 tablespoon olive oil
- 2 cloves garlic, minced

- 1 small red onion, finely chopped
- 2-3 bird's eye chilies, finely chopped (adjust to taste)
- 1 tablespoon roasted rice powder*
- 2 green onions, thinly sliced
- 1 handful chopped fresh coriander/cilantro
- 1 handful chopped fresh mint leaves
- Lettuce leaves, for serving
- Lime wedges, for serving

For the Roasted Rice Powder (optional):

- 2 tablespoons uncooked jasmine rice

Method:

1. To make the roasted rice powder, heat a dry skillet over medium heat. Add the uncooked jasmine rice and toast, stirring frequently, until golden brown and fragrant, about 5-7 minutes. Remove from heat and let cool. Once cooled, grind the toasted rice into a fine powder using a spice grinder or mortar and pestle. Set aside.
2. In a small bowl, mix together the fish sauce, lime juice, soy sauce, and honey to make the dressing. Set aside.
3. Heat the oil in a skillet over medium heat. Add the minced garlic and chopped red onion, and cook until softened, about 2-3 minutes.
4. Add the drained tuna to the skillet and break it up with a spoon. Cook for another 2-3 minutes, stirring occasionally.
5. Stir in the chopped Thai bird's eye chilies and roasted rice powder, and cook for another minute.
6. Pour the dressing over the tuna mixture and toss to combine. Cook for another 1-2 minutes to allow the flavours to meld together.
7. Remove from heat and transfer the spicy tuna larb to a

serving bowl.

8. Stir in the sliced green onions, chopped cilantro, and chopped mint leaves.
9. To serve, spoon the spicy tuna larb onto lettuce leaves. Garnish with additional chopped herbs and lime wedges on the side. This also works amazingly well on top of fresh salads.

Ras el Hanout Salmon

Ingredients:

- 4 salmon fillets
- Salt and black pepper to taste
- 2 tablespoons olive oil
- 2 tablespoons Ras el Hanout spice blend
- 2 cloves garlic, minced
- 1 tablespoon honey
- Zest and juice of 1 lemon
- Lemon wedges, for serving

Method:

1. Preheat your oven to 400°F (200°C). Line a baking sheet with parchment paper.
2. Pat the salmon fillets dry with paper towels and season them with salt and black pepper on both sides.
3. In a small bowl, mix together the olive oil, Ras el Hanout spice blend, minced garlic, honey, and lemon zest and juice to make a marinade.
4. Brush both sides of the salmon fillets with the marinade, ensuring they are well coated.
5. Place the salmon fillets on the prepared baking sheet.
6. Bake in the preheated oven for 12-15 minutes, or until the salmon is cooked through and flakes easily with a fork.
7. Once done, remove the salmon from the oven and transfer them to a serving platter.
8. Serve with lemon wedges on the side.

Curried Cod Wraps

Ingredients:

- 4 cod fillets
- Salt and black pepper to taste
- 2 tablespoons olive oil
- 2 tablespoons curry powder
- 1 teaspoon ground cumin
- 1 teaspoon ground coriander
- 1/2 teaspoon turmeric
- 1/2 teaspoon paprika
- 1/4 teaspoon cayenne pepper (adjust to taste)
- Juice of 1 lemon
- 4 large flour tortillas (either homemade, see our recipe, or we use Crosta & Mollica brand)
- 1 handful shredded lettuce
- 1 cucumber, thinly sliced
- 1 ripe tomato, thinly sliced
- Greek yoghurt for serving
- Fresh coriander/cilantro, chopped, for garnish

Method:

1. Preheat your grill or grill pan to medium-high heat.
2. Season the cod fillets with salt and black pepper on both sides.
3. In a small bowl, mix together the olive oil, curry powder, ground cumin, ground coriander, turmeric, paprika, cayenne pepper, and lemon juice to make a marinade.
4. Brush both sides of the cod fillets with the marinade, ensuring they are well coated.
5. Place the cod fillets on the preheated grill or grill pan.
6. Grill the cod fillets for 3-4 minutes on each side, or until they are cooked through and have nice grill

marks.

7. Once done, remove the cod fillets from the grill and transfer them to a cutting board. Let them rest for a few minutes, then flake them into bite-sized pieces using a fork.
8. Warm the flour tortillas according to package instructions.
9. To assemble the wraps, place a spoonful of shredded lettuce on each tortilla. Top with slices of cucumber and tomato.
10. Divide the flaked cod evenly among the tortillas, placing it on top of the vegetables.
11. If desired, add a dollop of Greek yoghurt on top of the cod.
12. Sprinkle with chopped fresh cilantro for garnish.
13. Roll up the tortillas to form wraps.

Prawns Pil Pil

Ingredients:

- 450g large prawns, peeled and deveined
- 4 cloves garlic, thinly sliced
- 1-2 red chilli peppers, thinly sliced (adjust to taste)
- 6 tablespoons olive oil, not extra virgin
- 2 tablespoons fresh parsley, chopped
- Juice of 1 lemon
- Salt to taste

Method:

1. Preheat your oven to 400°F (200°C).
2. In a frying pan or skillet , heat the olive oil over medium heat.
3. Add the sliced garlic and chilli peppers to the skillet and cook for 1-2 minutes, or until the garlic is fragrant and lightly golden.
4. Add the prawns to the skillet in a single layer. Cook for 1-2 minutes on each side, or until they turn pink and are just cooked through.
5. Remove the skillet from the heat and sprinkle the chopped parsley over the prawns.
6. Squeeze the lemon juice over the prawns and season with salt to taste.
7. Place the skillet back onto the heat for a minute until the prawns are sizzling and bubbling. Great served hot but also works well to top salads or in bread.

Curried Mango Prawns

Ingredients:

- 450g large prawns, peeled and deveined
- 1 ripe mango, peeled and diced
- 1 small onion, finely chopped
- 2 cloves garlic, minced
- 1 tablespoon curry powder
- 1 teaspoon ground turmeric
- 1 teaspoon ground cumin
- 1/2 teaspoon ground coriander
- 1/4 teaspoon cayenne pepper (adjust to taste)
- ½ 400g tin coconut milk
- Juice of 1 lime
- Salt and black pepper to taste
- 2 tablespoons olive oil
- Fresh coriander/cilantro, chopped, for garnish

Method:

1. In a large pan or skillet, heat the olive oil over medium heat.
2. Add the chopped onion to the skillet and cook until softened and translucent, about 3-4 minutes.
3. Stir in the minced garlic, curry powder, ground turmeric, ground cumin, ground coriander, and cayenne pepper. Cook for another 1-2 minutes, stirring constantly, until fragrant.
4. Add the diced mango to the skillet and cook for 2-3 minutes, stirring occasionally, until the mango starts to soften.
5. Pour in the coconut milk and bring the mixture to a simmer.
6. Add the peeled and deveined prawns to the skillet and cook for 5-6 minutes, or until the prawns are pink and cooked

through.

7. Stir in the lime juice and season with salt and black pepper to taste.
8. Once done, remove the skillet from the heat and garnish with chopped fresh cilantro.

Prawn Tacos with Mango Coriander Salsa

Ingredients:

For the Prawns:

- 450g large prawns, peeled and deveined
- 1 tablespoon olive oil
- 2 cloves garlic, minced

- 1 teaspoon ground cumin
- 1 teaspoon smoked paprika
- 1/2 teaspoon chilli powder
- Salt and black pepper to taste
- 8 small tortillas, we either make yoghurt flatbreads or use Crosta & Mollica brand

For the Mango Coriander Salsa:

- 1 ripe mango, peeled and diced
- ½ red onion, finely chopped
- 1 handful fresh coriander/cilantro, chopped
- Juice of 1 lime
- Salt and black pepper to taste

For Serving:

- Sour cream or Greek yoghurt
- Lime wedges
- Additional fresh coriander (cilantro), chopped

Method:

1. In a bowl, combine the peeled and deveined prawns with olive oil, minced garlic, ground cumin, smoked paprika, chilli powder, salt, and black pepper. Toss to coat the prawns evenly with the spices. Let marinate for 15-30 minutes.
2. While the prawns are marinating, prepare the mango coriander salsa. In another bowl, combine the diced mango, chopped red onion, chopped coriander, lime juice, salt, and black pepper. Mix well and set aside.
3. Heat a frying pan or skillet over medium-high heat.

Add the marinated prawns to the skillet and cook for 2-3 minutes on each side, or until they are pink and cooked through.

4. Warm the tortillas according to package instructions.
5. To assemble the tacos, place some cooked prawns in the centre of each tortilla. Top with a spoonful of mango coriander salsa.
6. Garnish the tacos with a dollop of sour cream or Greek yoghurt, additional fresh coriander (cilantro), and a squeeze of lime juice.

Garlic and Turmeric Squid Rings

Ingredients:

- 450g squid tubes, cleaned and cut into rings
- 3 cloves garlic, minced
- 1 teaspoon turmeric
- 2 tablespoons olive oil
- 1 tablespoon lemon juice
- Salt and black pepper to taste
- 2 tablespoons fresh parsley, chopped
- Lemon wedges, for serving

Method:

1. Pat the squid rings dry with paper towels and season them with salt and black pepper.
2. Heat the olive oil in a large frying pan or skillet over medium heat.
3. Add the minced garlic and turmeric to the skillet and cook for 1-2 minutes, or until fragrant.
4. Turn the heat up to high and the squid rings to the skillet in a single layer. Cook for 1-2 minutes on each side, or until they are opaque and cooked through.
5. Once done, remove the skillet from the heat and sprinkle the lemon juice and chopped fresh parsley over the squid rings. Toss to coat evenly.
6. Transfer the garlic squid rings to a serving platter.
7. Serve hot with lemon wedges on the side.

Mains - Beef

Peppercorn and Cumin Crusted Steak

Ingredients:

- 4 steak cuts of your choice (e.g., ribeye, sirloin)
- 2 tablespoons black peppercorns, crushed
- 1 teaspoon of cumin seeds, crushed
- 1 tablespoon olive oil
- Salt to taste
- 2 tablespoons butter
- 2 cloves garlic, minced
- Fresh thyme or rosemary sprigs

Method:

1. Preheat your frying pan to a very high heat.
2. Rub the steaks with olive oil and season with salt.
3. Press the crushed peppercorns and cumin onto both sides of the steaks.
4. Grill the steaks for 3-5 minutes on each side for medium-rare, or until cooked to your desired doneness. Avoid moving them around the pan, simply turn halfway through. Remove and allow to rest while you make the butter.
5. In the pan over medium heat, melt the butter and get all the brown pan bits leftover from the steak mixed in. Add the minced garlic and herbs and cook for 1 minute ensuring it doesn't burn.
6. Serve the steaks sliced with the garlic butter sauce drizzled on top.

Chimichurri Steak

Ingredients:

- 4 steak cuts of your choice, we like to use sirloin for this
- Salt and black pepper to taste
- 1 cup fresh parsley, chopped
- 1 handful fresh coriander/cilantro, chopped
- 3 cloves garlic, minced
- 1 tablespoon red wine vinegar
- 1 tablespoon olive oil
- 1 teaspoon dried oregano
- 1/2 teaspoon chilli flakes or fresh sliced chilli (optional)

Method:

1. Season the steaks generously with salt and black pepper.
2. In a blender or food processor, combine the parsley, coriander, minced garlic, red wine vinegar, olive oil, dried oregano, and chilli. Blend until smooth.
3. Marinate the steaks in half of the chimichurri sauce for at least 30 minutes, or overnight in the refrigerator.
4. Preheat your frying pan to a high heat.
5. Grill the steaks for 3-5 minutes on each side, or until cooked to your desired doneness.
6. Serve the grilled steaks with the remaining chimichurri sauce spooned over the top.

Balsamic Glazed Steak

Ingredients:

- 4 steak cuts of your choice, we like to use rump for this
- Salt and black pepper to taste
- 2 tablespoons balsamic vinegar
- 2 tablespoons honey
- 2 tablespoons soy sauce
- 2 cloves garlic, minced
- 1 tablespoon olive oil
- Fresh parsley, chopped, for garnish

Method:

1. Season the steaks with salt and black pepper.
2. In a small bowl, whisk together the balsamic vinegar, honey, soy sauce, and minced garlic to make the glaze.
3. Heat olive oil in a skillet over medium-high heat.
4. Add the steaks to the skillet and cook for 3-5 minutes on each side, or until cooked to your desired doneness.
5. Pour the balsamic glaze over the steaks and cook for an additional minute, allowing the glaze to thicken.
6. Garnish the steaks with chopped fresh parsley before serving.

Sliced Steak with Lime and Honey Dressing

Ingredients:

- 1 steaks of choice (we like to use rump for this)
- Salt and black pepper to taste
- 2 tablespoons olive oil
- 2 limes, juiced
- Zest of 1 lime
- 2 tablespoons honey
- 2 cloves garlic, minced
- 1 tablespoon soy sauce
- 1 tablespoon fresh coriander/cilantro, chopped (optional)
- Lime wedges, for serving
- Fresh coriander/cilantro leaves, for garnish

Method:

1. Season the steak generously with salt and black pepper on both sides.
2. In a bowl, whisk together the olive oil, lime juice, lime zest, honey, minced garlic, soy sauce, and chopped coriander/cilantro (if using) to make the dressing.
3. Place the steak in a shallow dish or resealable plastic bag. Pour half of the dressing over the steak, ensuring it's evenly coated. Reserve the remaining dressing for serving.
4. Marinate the steak in the refrigerator for at least 30 minutes, or up to 2 hours.
5. Preheat your grill or grill pan to medium-high heat.
6. Remove the steak from the marinade and discard the excess marinade.
7. Grill the steak for 4-5 minutes on each side for medium-rare, or until cooked to your desired doneness.
8. Once done, transfer the steak to a cutting board and let it rest for a few minutes.
9. Slice the steak thinly against the grain.

10. Arrange the sliced steak on a serving platter.
11. Drizzle the reserved lime and honey dressing over the sliced steak.
12. Garnish with fresh cilantro leaves and serve hot with lime wedges on the side.

Mains - Veggie

Mediterranean Halloumi Bake

Ingredients:

- 500g halloumi cheese, sliced
- 2 large aubergines (eggplant), sliced into rounds
- 2 large courgettes (zucchini), sliced into rounds
- 1 fennel bulb, thinly sliced
- 2 tablespoons capers, drained

- 2 tablespoons olive oil
- 2 cloves garlic, minced
- 1 teaspoon dried oregano
- 1 teaspoon dried thyme
- Salt and pepper to taste
- Olive oil for greasing dish
- 500g can or bottles of passata
- Lemon wedges for serving

Instructions:

1. Preheat your oven to 200°C (400°F). Place the sliced aubergine, courgette, and fennel in a large roasting dish that's been drizzled with olive oil. Drizzle with olive oil, minced garlic, dried oregano, dried thyme, salt, and pepper. Toss well to coat the vegetables evenly. Pour over the passata and season, then bake for 25 minutes.

3. Place the sliced halloumi on top of the vegetables and scatter the capers over the top. Bake for a further 15-20 minutes, or until the vegetables are tender and the halloumi is golden brown and slightly crispy on top.

Lemon, Tomato & Cardamom Dhal

Ingredients:

- 200g red lentils
- 400ml water
- 2 tablespoons olive oil
- 1 onion, finely chopped
- 3 cloves garlic, minced
- 1-inch piece of ginger, grated (from frozen works well)
- 2 large tomatoes, diced
- 1 teaspoon ground turmeric
- 1 teaspoon ground cumin
- 1 teaspoon ground coriander
- 1/2 teaspoon ground cardamom or 5 whole pods gently crushed
- 1/4 teaspoon cayenne or chilli pepper (optional)
- Juice and zest of 2 lemons
- Salt to taste
- Fresh coriander/cilantro leaves, chopped, for garnish

Method:

1. Rinse the red lentils under cold water until the water runs clear. Drain well.
2. In a large saucepan, combine the lentils and water. Bring to a boil over medium-high heat.
3. Reduce the heat to low and simmer the lentils, partially covered, for about 20 minutes or until tender. Stir occasionally and add more water if needed to prevent sticking.
4. While the lentils are cooking, heat the olive oil in a separate skillet over medium heat.
5. Add the chopped onion to the skillet and sauté until softened and translucent.
6. Stir in the minced garlic and grated ginger, and cook for

another minute until fragrant.

7. Add the diced tomatoes to the skillet and cook until they begin to soften.
8. Stir in the ground turmeric, cumin, coriander, cardamom, and cayenne pepper (if using). Cook for another minute to toast the spices.
9. Once the lentils are tender, add the tomato mixture to the saucepan and stir to combine.
10. Cook the dhal for another 5-10 minutes, stirring occasionally, until the flavours meld together and the dhal reaches your desired consistency.
11. Stir in the lemon juice and zest. Season with salt to taste.

Pasta Frittata with Onion

Ingredients:

- 300g cooked pasta (spaghetti, rigatoni or any other pasta as this is a great way to use up leftovers)
- 1 medium onion, finely chopped
- 6 large eggs
- 100g mozzarella, diced
- 50g Parmesan, grated
- Salt and black pepper to taste
- 2 tbsp olive oil

Instructions:

1. In a large frying pan, heat 1 tablespoon of olive oil over medium heat. Add the chopped onion and cook until soft and translucent, about 5-7 minutes. Remove from the pan and set aside.
2. In a large bowl, beat the eggs. Add the diced mozzarella, grated Parmesan, cooked onion, and a pinch of salt and black pepper. Mix well.
3. Add the cooked pasta to the bowl with the egg mixture and mix until the pasta is well coated.
4. Heat the remaining tablespoon of olive oil in the frying pan over medium heat. Pour the pasta and egg mixture into the pan, spreading it out evenly. Cook for about 5-7 minutes until the bottom is set and golden.
5. Place the pan under a preheated grill for another 5 minutes, or until the top is set and golden brown. Allow the frittata to cool slightly before slicing and serving.

Smoky Whole Aubergine

Ingredients:

- 2 medium aubergines (eggplants)
- 2 tablespoons olive oil
- 2 cloves garlic, minced
- 1 teaspoon smoked paprika
- 1/2 teaspoon ground cumin
- 1/2 teaspoon ground coriander
- Salt and black pepper to taste
- Fresh parsley or coriander/cilantro leaves, chopped, for garnish (optional)
- Lemon wedges, for serving

Method:

1. Preheat your grill to medium-high heat.
2. Wash the aubergines and pat them dry with a paper towel. Pierce each aubergine several times with a fork to prevent them from bursting while grilling.
3. In a small bowl, mix together the olive oil, minced garlic, smoked paprika, ground cumin, ground coriander, salt, and black pepper.
4. Brush the aubergines all over with the olive oil and spice mixture.
5. Place the aubergines directly on the grill grate and cook for 20-25 minutes, turning occasionally, until the skin is charred and the flesh is soft and tender.
6. Remove the grilled aubergines from the grill and transfer them to a serving platter.
7. Slice the aubergines open lengthwise and fluff the flesh with a fork.
8. Sprinkle with chopped fresh parsley or coriander leaves, if desired, and serve hot with lemon wedges on the side.

Cheesy Spinach Terrine (Sformato di Spinaci)

Ingredients:

- 500g fresh spinach leaves, washed and trimmed
- 1 tablespoon butter
- 1 small onion, finely chopped
- 2 cloves garlic, minced
- 200g ricotta cheese
- 100g grated Parmesan cheese
- 2 eggs, beaten
- 100ml milk
- Salt and black pepper to taste
- Pinch of nutmeg
- Butter, for greasing the pan
- Breadcrumbs, for coating the pan (we use crushed Crosta & Mollica breadsticks if we don't have any stale bread in the house but semolina works well too)
- Extra grated Parmesan cheese, for topping

Method:

1. Preheat your oven to 180°C (350°F). Grease a terrine dish or loaf pan with butter and coat it with breadcrumbs, tapping out any excess.
2. Bring a large pot of salted water to a boil. Add the spinach leaves and blanch for 1-2 minutes until wilted. Drain the spinach and rinse under cold water to stop the cooking process. Squeeze out any excess moisture and chop the spinach finely.
3. In a skillet, melt the butter over medium heat. Add the finely chopped onion and minced garlic, and sauté until softened and translucent.
4. In a large mixing bowl, combine the chopped spinach, sautéed onion and garlic, ricotta cheese, grated Parmesan cheese, beaten eggs, milk, salt, black pepper, and nutmeg.

Mix well to combine all the ingredients.

5. Pour the spinach mixture into the prepared terrine dish or loaf pan. Smooth the top with a spatula and sprinkle extra grated Parmesan cheese on top.
6. Place the terrine dish or loaf pan in a larger baking dish. Pour hot water into the larger baking dish to create a water bath (bain-marie) around the terrine dish or loaf pan. This will help the terrine cook evenly and prevent it from cracking.
7. Bake in the preheated oven for 45-50 minutes, or until the terrine is set and golden brown on top.
8. Remove the terrine from the oven and let it cool for at least 15-20 minutes before slicing.

Lentil Loaf

Ingredients:

- 200g dried brown lentils
- 400ml water
- 2 tablespoons olive oil
- 1 onion, finely chopped
- 2 cloves garlic, minced
- 2 carrots, grated
- 1 celery stalk, finely chopped
- 1 red pepper, finely chopped
- 100g breadcrumbs (we use bashed Crosta & Mollica breadsticks if we don't have any stale bread in the house)
- 50g rolled oats
- 30g tomato paste
- 2 tablespoons soy sauce
- 1 teaspoon dried thyme
- 1 teaspoon dried oregano
- 1/2 teaspoon smoked paprika
- Salt and black pepper to taste

Method:

1. Preheat your oven to 180°C (350°F). Grease a loaf pan with olive oil or line it with parchment paper.
2. Rinse the lentils under cold water and drain well. In a saucepan, bring the vegetable broth or water to a boil. Add the lentils, reduce the heat to low, cover, and simmer for 20-25 minutes, or until the lentils are tender and the liquid is absorbed. Remove from heat and let cool slightly.
3. In a large frying pan or skillet, heat the olive oil over medium heat. Add the chopped onion and garlic, and sauté until softened and translucent.
4. Add the grated carrot, chopped celery, and pepper to

the skillet. Cook for another 5-7 minutes, or until the vegetables are tender.

5. In a large mixing bowl, combine the cooked lentils, sautéed vegetables, breadcrumbs, rolled oats, tomato paste, soy sauce, dried thyme, dried oregano, smoked paprika, salt, and black pepper. Mix well to combine all the ingredients.
6. Transfer the lentil mixture to the prepared loaf pan and press it down firmly with the back of a spoon or your hands.
7. Bake in the preheated oven for 40-45 minutes, or until the lentil loaf is firm and golden brown on top.
8. Remove the lentil loaf from the oven and let it cool in the pan for 10-15 minutes before slicing.

Not the Usual Devilled Eggs

Ingredients:

- 6 large eggs
- 2 tablespoons creme fraiche
- ½ teaspoon smoked paprika
- 1 teaspoon capers, chopped
- 1 teaspoon white vinegar or lemon juice
- 1/4 teaspoon salt
- 1/4 teaspoon black pepper
- Paprika, for garnish
- Fresh chives or parsley, chopped, for garnish (optional)

Method:

1. Place the eggs in a saucepan and cover them with cold water. Bring the water to a boil over medium-high heat.
2. Once the water reaches a rolling boil, reduce the heat to low and let the eggs simmer for 10 minutes.
3. After 10 minutes, remove the saucepan from the heat and carefully transfer the eggs to a bowl of ice water to cool completely. As you do this, bash the bottom of the eggs on the bowl to crack the shell slightly. This will stop the cooking process and make the eggs easier to peel.
4. Once the eggs are cool, carefully peel off the shells and discard them.
5. Slice each egg in half lengthwise, and gently scoop out the yolks into a small bowl. Arrange the egg white halves on a serving platter.
6. Mash the egg yolks with a fork until they are smooth and crumbly.
7. Add the creme fraiche, smoked paprika, capers, white vinegar or lemon juice, salt, and black pepper to the mashed egg yolks. Stir until well combined and creamy.
8. Spoon or pipe the egg yolk mixture back into the hollows of

the egg white halves, dividing it evenly among them.

9. Sprinkle a pinch of paprika over each devilled egg for garnish.
10. If desired, garnish the devilled eggs with chopped fresh chives or parsley for added flavour and colour.

Flamiche

Ingredients:

For the pastry:

- 150g plain all-purpose flour
- 1/2 teaspoon salt
- 115g cold unsalted butter, diced
- 60ml ice water

For the filling:

- 2 tablespoons unsalted butter
- 2 large leeks, white and light green parts only, thinly sliced
- Salt and black pepper to taste

- 100g grated Gruyère cheese
- 150ml double cream
- 2 large eggs
- Pinch of nutmeg (optional)
- Chopped fresh chives or parsley for garnish (optional)

Method:

1. Prepare the pastry:

In a large mixing bowl, whisk together the flour and salt. Add the diced butter to the flour mixture and use a pastry cutter or your fingertips to rub the butter into the flour until the mixture resembles coarse crumbs. Gradually add the ice water, 1 tablespoon at a time, mixing until the dough comes together. Shape the dough into a disc, wrap it in plastic wrap, and refrigerate for at least 30 minutes.

2. Preheat the oven and prepare filling:

Preheat your oven to 200°C (400°F).

In a pan or skillet, melt the butter over medium heat. Add the sliced leeks and cook, stirring occasionally, until softened, about 8-10 minutes. Season with salt and black pepper to taste. Remove from heat and let cool slightly. In a mixing bowl, whisk together the heavy cream, eggs, and pinch of nutmeg (if using).

3. Assemble the Flamiche:

On a lightly floured surface, roll out the chilled pastry dough into a circle about 12 inches in diameter. Transfer the rolled-out dough to a tart pan or pie dish, pressing it gently into the bottom and up the sides. Trim any excess dough hanging over the edges.

Spread the cooked leeks evenly over the bottom of the pastry crust. Sprinkle the grated Gruyère cheese over the leeks. Pour the cream and egg mixture over the leeks and cheese.

4. Bake and serve:

Place the tart pan or pie dish on a baking sheet and transfer it to the preheated oven. Bake for 25-30 minutes, or until the pastry is golden brown and the filling is set. Remove the Flamiche from the oven and let it cool for a few minutes before slicing. Garnish the Flamiche with chopped fresh chives or parsley, if desired.

Quick Pickled Eggs

Ingredients:

- 6 hard-boiled eggs, peeled
- 100ml white or malt vinegar
- 100ml water
- 2 tablespoons granulated sugar
- 1 tablespoon salt
- 1 teaspoon whole black peppercorns
- 2 cloves garlic, smashed (optional)
- 1 bay leaf (optional)
- 1 teaspoon mustard seeds (optional)
- 1 teaspoon red chilli flakes (optional)
- Fresh dill sprigs (optional)

Method:

1. Prepare the Pickling Solution:
   - In a saucepan, combine the white vinegar, water, sugar, salt, whole black peppercorns, garlic cloves, bay leaf, mustard seeds, and red pepper flakes (if using). Bring the mixture to a boil over medium heat, stirring occasionally until the sugar and salt are dissolved. Remove the saucepan from the heat and let the pickling solution cool to room temperature.
2. Pickling the Eggs:
   - Place the peeled hard-boiled eggs in a clean glass jar or container large enough to hold them.
   - Once the pickling solution has cooled, pour it over the eggs, making sure they are completely submerged. If desired, add fresh dill sprigs for extra flavour.
   - Seal the jar or container with a tight-fitting lid and refrigerate for at least 24 hours to allow the flavours to develop. The longer you let the eggs pickle, the more flavorful they will become. Store any leftovers in

the refrigerator in an airtight container for up to 1-2 weeks.

Extras - Pasta Sauces and Dips

Tomato, Mascarpone, and Capers Sauce

Ingredients:

- 100g tomato puree
- 100g cup mascarpone cheese
- 2 tablespoons capers, chopped

- 2 cloves garlic, minced
- 2 tablespoons olive oil
- Salt and black pepper to taste
- Grated Parmesan cheese, for serving
- Fresh basil leaves, chopped, for garnish (optional)

Method:

1. In a large skillet, heat the olive oil over medium heat. Add the minced garlic and cook for 1-2 minutes, or until fragrant.
2. Stir in the tomato puree and cook for 3-4 minutes, stirring occasionally.
3. Add the mascarpone cheese to the skillet and stir until it melts and combines with the tomato puree to form a creamy sauce.
4. Stir in the chopped capers and season the sauce with salt and black pepper to taste.

Classic Marinara Sauce

Ingredients:

- 400g tin chopped tomatoes
- 2 tablespoons tomato paste
- 2 cloves garlic, minced
- 1 small onion, finely chopped
- 2 tablespoons olive oil
- 1 teaspoon dried oregano
- 1 teaspoon dried basil
- Salt and black pepper to taste
- Pinch of sugar (optional)

Method:

1. Heat olive oil in a saucepan over medium heat. Add minced garlic and chopped onion, and cook until softened.
2. Stir in tomato paste and cook for 1-2 minutes.
3. Add chopped tomatoes, dried oregano, dried basil, salt, black pepper, and sugar (if using). Bring to a simmer.
4. Reduce heat to low and let the sauce simmer for about 20-25 minutes, stirring occasionally, until thickened.

Super Simple Pesto

Ingredients:

- 50g fresh basil leaves
- 50g pine nuts
- 50g grated Parmesan cheese
- 2 cloves garlic
- 100ml extra virgin olive oil
- Salt and black pepper to taste
- Lemon, optional

Method:

1. In a food processor or pestle and mortar, combine pine nuts, grated Parmesan cheese, and garlic cloves. Pulse or bash until finely chopped.
2. Add the basil and if with the food processor running, slowly drizzle in the extra virgin olive oil until the mixture forms a smooth paste.
3. Season with salt and black pepper to taste.
4. Toss the pesto sauce with your choice of cooked pasta until well coated. Adjust the consistency with a splash of pasta cooking water if needed.
5. Serve optionally garnished with extra grated Parmesan cheese and a squeeze and zest of lemon.

Mushroom and Cream Sauce

Ingredients:

- 250g chestnut mushrooms, sliced
- 2 cloves garlic, minced
- 1 small onion, finely chopped
- 2 tablespoons olive oil
- 200ml double cream
- Salt and black pepper to taste
- Zest and juice of 1 lemon
- Fresh parsley, chopped, for garnish (optional)

Method:

1. Heat olive oil in a large skillet over medium heat. Add minced garlic and chopped onion, and cook until softened.
2. Add sliced mushrooms to the skillet and cook until they release their juices and turn golden brown.
3. Pour in double cream and bring to a simmer. Cook for about 5-7 minutes, stirring occasionally, until the sauce thickens slightly. Add in the lemon.
4. Season with salt and black pepper to taste. Adjust consistency with a splash of pasta cooking water if needed.
5. Serve over cooked pasta, garnished with chopped fresh parsley if desired.

Roasted Red Pepper and Red Wine Sauce

Ingredients:

- 3 large red bell peppers
- 2 cloves garlic, minced
- 2 tablespoons olive oil
- 75ml red wine
- 1 tablespoon balsamic vinegar
- Pinch of sugar or ½ teaspoon honey
- 50g grated Parmesan cheese
- Salt and black pepper to taste
- Fresh basil leaves, chopped, for garnish (optional)

Method:

1. Preheat your grill to high heat. Place red bell peppers on a baking sheet and grill, turning occasionally, until charred and blistered on all sides.
2. Transfer the grilled peppers to a bowl, cover with plastic wrap, and let them steam for about 10 minutes. Then, remove the skins, seeds, and stems from the peppers.
3. In a blender or food processor, combine the grilled peppers, minced garlic, olive oil, wine, vinegar, sugar or honey and grated Parmesan cheese. Blend until smooth.
4. Transfer the sauce to a saucepan and heat over medium heat until warmed through. Season with salt and black pepper to taste.

Puttanesca-ish

Ingredients:

- 2 tbsp olive oil
- 4 cloves garlic, minced
- 2 anchovy fillets, finely chopped (optional)
- 2 red chillies, finely chopped
- 1 400g tin chopped tomatoes
- 2 tbsp capers, rinsed and drained
- 2 tbsp fresh parsley, chopped
- Salt and pepper to taste
- Grated Parmesan cheese and squeeze of lemon (optional), for serving

Instructions:

1. In a large pan or skillet, heat the olive oil over medium heat. Add the minced garlic and anchovy fillets (if using) and sauté for 1-2 minutes until fragrant.
2. Add the chopped red chillies to the skillet and cook for another minute.
3. Pour in the chopped tomatoes and bring the sauce to a simmer. Let it cook for about 10 minutes, stirring occasionally, until the sauce has thickened slightly.
4. Stir in the capers, and cook for another 2-3 minutes.
5. Season the sauce with salt, pepper and lemon juice to taste. Remember that capers are salty, so adjust the salt accordingly.

Pea and Mint "Pesto"

Ingredients:

- 200g frozen peas, thawed
- 50g fresh mint leaves
- 50g grated Parmesan cheese (or feta works well too)
- 2 cloves garlic, minced
- Juice of 1 lemon
- Zest of 1 lemon
- 60ml olive oil
- Salt and pepper to taste

Instructions:

1. If you haven't already done so, thaw the frozen peas by placing them in a bowl of warm water for a few minutes. Drain them well.
2. In a food processor, combine the thawed peas, fresh mint leaves, grated Parmesan cheese, minced garlic, lemon juice, and lemon zest. Pulse until the mixture is roughly chopped and well combined.
3. With the food processor running, slowly drizzle in the olive oil until the pesto reaches your desired consistency. You may need to scrape down the sides of the food processor bowl with a spatula occasionally to ensure everything is well incorporated.
4. Season the pea and mint pesto with salt and pepper to taste. Remember that the Parmesan cheese adds saltiness, so adjust the seasoning accordingly.
5. Transfer the pesto to a jar or airtight container and store it in the refrigerator until ready to use. It can be kept for up to a week.

Ricotta Sauce with Garlic and Pistachios

Ingredients:

- 250g ricotta cheese
- 2 cloves garlic, minced
- 50g shelled pistachios, toasted in a dry pan and roughly chopped
- Zest of 1 lemon
- Juice of 1 lemon
- 2-3 tablespoons extra virgin olive oil
- Salt and pepper to taste
- Fresh basil leaves, torn, for garnish (optional)

Instructions:

1. In a small saucepan, heat the olive oil over medium heat. Add the minced garlic and sauté for 1-2 minutes until fragrant. Be careful not to let it brown.
2. In a mixing bowl, combine the ricotta cheese, minced garlic, chopped pistachios, lemon zest, and lemon juice. Stir until well combined.
3. Gradually add the olive oil to the ricotta mixture, stirring continuously until the sauce reaches a smooth and creamy consistency. You may need to adjust the amount of olive oil based on your desired thickness.
4. Season the ricotta sauce with salt and pepper to taste and garnish with torn fresh basil leaves, if desired, before serving.

Roasted Cherry Tomato Sauce with Zesty Orange

Ingredients:

- 500g cherry tomatoes
- 4 cloves garlic, minced
- 2 tablespoons olive oil
- Salt and pepper to taste
- Zest and juice of 1 orange
- Fresh basil leaves, torn, for garnish

Instructions:

1. Preheat your oven to 180°C.
2. Place the cherry tomatoes on a baking sheet lined with parchment paper. Drizzle them with olive oil and sprinkle minced garlic over the top. Season with salt and pepper to taste.
3. Roast the cherry tomatoes in the preheated oven for about 20-25 minutes, or until they are soft and slightly caramelised.
4. If you like a chunky sauce, once the cherry tomatoes are done roasting simply mash lightly in the pan. For a smoother sauce, transfer them to a blender or food processor and blend until smooth.
5. Pour the blended tomato sauce back into the pan and heat it over medium heat. Stir in the zest and juice of one orange and let the sauce simmer for a few minutes to allow the flavours to meld together.

Miso Aioli Style Dip

Ingredients:

- 100ml sour cream or mascarpone
- 2 cloves garlic, minced
- 1 teaspoon miso paste (we like Yutaka brand)

Instructions:

1. Simply mix and enjoy!

Extras - Breads

The Best Yogurt Flatbread

Ingredients:

- 250g plain flour (plus extra for dusting)
- 200g Greek or natural yoghurt
- 1 teaspoon baking powder
- 1/2 teaspoon salt
- 2 tablespoons olive oil (plus extra for brushing)

Instructions:

1. Prepare the Dough:

1. In a large mixing bowl, combine the plain flour, baking powder, and salt.
2. Add the greek yoghurt and olive oil to the dry ingredients.
3. Mix the ingredients together using a spoon or your hands until a dough starts to form.

2. Knead the Dough:

1. Transfer the dough to a clean, floured surface.
2. Knead the dough for about 5-7 minutes until it becomes smooth and elastic.
3. If the dough feels too sticky, you can add a little more flour as needed.

3. Rest the Dough:

1. Shape the dough into a ball and place it back into the mixing bowl.
2. Cover the bowl with a clean kitchen towel or cling film.
3. Let the dough rest for at least 30 minutes at room temperature. This will allow the gluten to relax and make the dough easier to work with.

4. Divide and Roll Out the Dough:

1. After resting, divide the dough into small balls, roughly the size of a golf ball.
2. On a floured surface, roll out each dough ball into a thin circle, about 1/8 inch thick. You can use a rolling pin for this.
3. If the dough starts to shrink back, let it rest for a few minutes and then continue rolling.

5. Cook the Flatbreads:

1. Heat a non-stick skillet or frying pan over medium-high heat.
2. Once the pan is hot, place a rolled-out flatbread onto it.
3. Cook for about 1-2 minutes on each side, or until golden brown spots appear and the bread puffs up.
4. Brush each side with a little olive oil while cooking for extra flavor and moisture.
5. Transfer the cooked flatbread to a plate and cover with a clean kitchen towel to keep warm while you cook the remaining flatbreads.

Cheese and Onion Soda Bread

Ingredients:

- 300g plain flour
- 1 teaspoon baking soda
- 1 teaspoon salt
- 150g grated cheddar cheese
- 1 small red onion, finely chopped
- 250ml buttermilk
- 1 tablespoon olive oil
- Extra cheese for topping (optional)
- Extra chopped onion for topping (optional)

Instructions:

1. Preheat the Oven:

Preheat your oven to 200°C (180°C fan/ gas mark 6). Line a baking tray with parchment paper or lightly grease it with oil.

2. Prepare the Dough:

In a large mixing bowl, sift together the plain flour and baking soda. Stir in the salt, grated cheddar cheese, and chopped onion until evenly distributed. Make a well in the centre of the dry ingredients and pour in the buttermilk. Using a wooden spoon or your hands, mix everything together lightly until a rough dough forms.

3. Knead the Dough:

Transfer the dough onto a floured surface. Knead the dough lightly for a minute or two until it comes together and is no longer sticky. Shape the dough into a round loaf.

4. Score and Top the Loaf:

Place the shaped loaf onto the prepared baking tray. Using a sharp knife, score a deep cross on top of the loaf, about 2cm deep.

If desired, sprinkle extra grated cheese and chopped onion on top of the loaf for extra flavour and decoration.

5. Bake the Bread:

Place the baking tray in the preheated oven and bake for 30-35 minutes, or until the bread is golden brown and sounds hollow when tapped on the bottom. If the bread starts to brown too quickly, you can cover it loosely with foil halfway through baking. Once baked, transfer the bread to a wire rack to cool slightly before slicing.

Simple Tortilla Wraps:

Ingredients:

- 250g plain flour
- 1 teaspoon salt
- 2 tablespoons olive oil
- 150ml warm water

Instructions:

1. Mixing the Dough:

In a large mixing bowl, combine the plain flour and salt. Make a well in the centre of the dry ingredients and add the oil and warm water. Use a wooden spoon or your hands to mix everything together until a rough dough forms.

2. Kneading the Dough:

Transfer the dough onto a lightly floured surface. Knead the dough for about 5-7 minutes until it becomes smooth and elastic. If the dough is too sticky, you can add a little more flour as needed.

3. Resting the Dough:

Shape the dough into a ball and place it back into the mixing bowl. Cover the bowl with a clean kitchen towel or cling film. Let the dough rest for at least 15-30 minutes at room temperature. This allows the gluten to relax and makes the dough easier to roll out.

4. Dividing and Rolling Out the Dough:

After resting, divide the dough into 6 equal portions. On a floured surface, roll out each portion of dough into a thin circle, about 8-10 inches in diameter. You can use a rolling pin or tortilla press for this. If the dough starts to shrink back, let it rest for a few minutes and then continue rolling.

5. Cooking the Tortilla Wraps:

Heat a non-stick skillet or frying pan over medium-high heat. Once the pan is hot, place a rolled-out tortilla onto it. Cook for about 1-2 minutes on each side, or until lightly golden brown spots appear and the tortilla puffs up slightly. Repeat with the remaining tortillas, stacking them on a plate as they are cooked.

Savoury Cheese Scones:

Ingredients:

- 300g self-raising flour
- 1 teaspoon baking powder
- 1/2 teaspoon salt
- 50g unsalted butter, cold and cubed
- 150g grated cheddar cheese
- 1 small onion, finely chopped
- 2 tablespoons chopped fresh herbs (such as chives, parsley, or thyme)
- 150ml milk
- 1 large egg, beaten (for egg wash)

Instructions:

1. Preheat the Oven:

Preheat your oven to 220°C (200°C fan/ gas mark 7). Line a baking tray with parchment paper or lightly grease it with oil.

2. Prepare the Dry Ingredients:

In a large mixing bowl, sift together the self-raising flour, baking powder, and salt.Add the cold cubed butter to the dry ingredients.

3. Incorporate the Butter:

Using your fingertips or a pastry cutter, rub the butter into the flour mixture until it resembles coarse breadcrumbs. Stir in the grated cheddar cheese, chopped onion, and fresh herbs until evenly distributed.

4. Combine the Wet Ingredients:

Make a well in the centre of the dry ingredients. Pour in the milk and gently mix until a soft dough forms. Be careful not to overmix.

5. Shape the Scones:

Transfer the dough onto a floured surface. Pat the dough into a circle about 2cm thick. Use a floured round cutter (about 6-7cm in diameter) to cut out scones from the dough. Place the scones onto the prepared baking tray, leaving a little space between each one.

6. Bake the Scones:

Brush the tops of the scones with beaten egg for a golden finish. Bake in the preheated oven for 12-15 minutes, or until the scones are risen and golden brown.

No-knead Overnight Bread

Ingredients:

- 500g strong white bread flour
- 1/4 teaspoon instant yeast (these may have some additives, but I tend to think of this as a far lesser evil than buying commercial bread)
- 1 1/2 teaspoons salt
- 350ml lukewarm water

Instructions:

1. Mixing the Dough:

In a large mixing bowl, combine the flour, instant yeast, and salt. Add the lukewarm water to the dry ingredients and mix until a shaggy dough forms. It's okay if it looks rough and sticky.

2. Resting the Dough:

Cover the bowl with plastic wrap or a clean kitchen towel. Let the dough rest at room temperature for 12-18 hours, overnight works well.

3. Preparing to Bake:

After the resting period, preheat your oven to 230°C (450°F). Place a tray of water in the bottom of the oven as it preheats to create steam which helps form a deep crust. While the oven is heating up, remove the plastic wrap or towel from the bowl.

4. Shaping the Dough:

Lightly flour your hands and a work surface. Gently scrape the dough out of the bowl onto the floured surface. Shape the dough into a ball by tucking the edges underneath, creating tension on the surface.

5. Baking the Bread:

1. Place the shaped dough into a dutch oven type pot or oven tray, seam side down.
2. If using a dutch oven type pot, cover the pot with the lid, and place it back into the oven.
3. Bake for 30 minutes with the lid on where applicable. After 30 minutes, remove the lid and bake for an additional 15-20 minutes, or until the bread is deeply golden brown and sounds hollow when tapped on the bottom.

Wholemeal Roti

Ingredients:

- 200g wholemeal flour
- 1/2 teaspoon salt
- 120ml warm water (approximately)

Instructions:

1. Mixing the Dough:

In a large mixing bowl, combine the wholemeal flour and salt. Gradually add warm water to the flour mixture, stirring with a spoon or your hands, until a soft dough forms. You may not need to use all of the water, or you may need a little more. The dough should be soft and pliable but not sticky.

2. Resting the Dough:

Once the dough comes together, knead it briefly for about 2-3 minutes on a clean surface until it becomes smooth. Shape the dough into a ball and cover it with a clean kitchen towel or plastic wrap. Let the dough rest for at least 15-20 minutes at room temperature. This allows the gluten to relax and makes the dough easier to roll out.

3. Rolling Out the Roti:

After resting, divide the dough into equal-sized portions, roughly the size of golf balls. Roll each portion into a smooth ball between your palms. On a lightly floured surface, flatten one dough ball with your palm. Using a rolling pin, roll out the dough into a thin circle, about 6-8 inches in diameter. Aim for an even thickness throughout.

4. Cooking the Roti:

Heat a non-stick skillet or tawa over medium-high heat. Once the skillet is hot, carefully transfer the rolled-out roti onto it.

Cook the roti for about 1-2 minutes on one side, or until you see small bubbles forming. Flip the roti and cook for another 1-2 minutes on the other side. You may need to press down gently with a spatula to help it cook evenly. Both sides should have light golden brown spots when done.

5. Serving:

Once cooked, transfer the roti to a plate and cover it with a clean kitchen towel to keep warm. Repeat the rolling and cooking process with the remaining dough balls.

Extras - Snacks

Here are some of the quickest to prepare snacks that can really hit the spot and require very little effort.

Nuts - toasted or untoasted but we love pecans that have been dry roasted in a frying pan with a mixed spice.

Portioned cheeses - Think little wedges of brie, cubes of cheddar, mini balls of mozzarella, slices of applewood all ready to go with a cracker or two. Cottage cheese also works well as a base for a savoury snack bowl e.g. topped with cherry tomatoes, basil and pine nuts.

Crackers - Matzo crackers along with some great brands like Crosta & Mollica or Peter's Yard make great ready made choices but you can also make your own very easily with just flour and water.

Rice cakes - The plain ones are often UPF free and a great go-to snack especially with 100% peanut butter and some fresh fruit.

Dried fruit - It can be hard to find these without sunflower oil but we find this acceptable in the great scheme of things considering the amount and the alternatives. However, there are also some brands such as Crazy Jacks who produce 100% dried organic fruit.

Natural yoghurt - Proper greek yoghurt with a drizzle of raw honey is always a winner in our house.

Cereal - Some cereal such as shredded wheat are non UPF and oats mixed with yoghurt makes a wonderful fridge ready bircher muesli for a grab and go snack.

100% nut butters - These are great tummy fillers and can be used in so many ways. We like almond butter on celery sticks with a few raisins on top (affectionately known as ants on a log).

Veggie sticks and fresh fruit - Sometimes the simplest ideas are the best and by having these prepared and ready to go in pots you may be more inclined to reach for them.

Toast with proper butter - I personally don't think life gets much better than this. If homemade bread isn't on the cards I go for Jason's brand as it is now widely available and UPF free. I store it in the freezer as it has a shorter shelf life than most supermarket breads for all the right reasons.

Boiled eggs - We batch make these and always have a jar in the fridge to grab for easy breakfasts or snacks.

Kale crisps - Even my kids love these! Simply scatter some shredded kale leaves on a baking tray and roast at 180 degrees celsius for around 5 minutes until crispy. I like to rub my hands with olive oil and scrunch this through the leaves before roasting with a sprinkle of sea salt.

Lacto-fermented pickles - A lot tastier than they sound! You can preserve most veggies in a brine made with 2% seasalt to the volume of water. We love cherry tomatoes as they go fizzy and burst, quite literally, with flavour on the tongue. Others include fermented carrot sticks and simple sauerkraut.

Milk kefir - This fermented and slightly fizzy milk drink has an extremely mild cheesiness to it that gives it a savoury twang. I find a small glass of this can really put hunger pangs to rest as it satisfies the need for flavour.

Chocolate - There are some brands out there flying the flag for reduced UPF, we like Hu and Willies Cacao as they skip the emulsifiers and extracts.